THE ZOO OF YOU

Learning to Walk Without Crutches, Transforming Defense Mechanisms into Life Skills

D1492974

BRENDA R. ABERCROMBIE, LPCC, LADAC

ISBN 979-8-89112-107-2 (Paperback)
ISBN 979-8-89112-108-9 (Digital)

Covenant Books
11661 Hwy 707
Murrells Inlet, SC 29576
www.covenantbooks.com

CONTENTS

PREFACE

Today, I retired from a twenty-eight-year counseling career. Now, at sixty-six years old, I'm facing my own mental health dilemma. My mind and heart are conflicted. I should be happy at this new juncture in my life. However, I have fears and reservations. This feels like a crisis, and I think I'm going to need some help to learn to adjust. Self-reflection tells me that I am the counselor, heal myself. I feel like a person with a broken leg that's healed but no knowledge of how to walk on the new leg. Crutches are no longer necessary, but the experience of walking without them feels awkward and unfamiliar. My training tells me that therapy heals. Today, I say yes to healing, recovery, and moving forward. I ask God to guide me because He has always been the best counselor from the beginning of time. Please join me on this therapeutic journey.

ACKNOWLEDGMENTS

For the past year and a half, writing this book has been part of my life. My family has helped me, redirected me, and encouraged me as I wrote and rewrote, edited and reedited page after page.

As I reflected on my childhood, I reached out to my parents and siblings. They helped me get some of my memories straight. They also helped me understand what my common defense mechanisms have been through the years.

My husband has been there for me, day after day, as I asked for feedback and sometimes got insights into myself that were surprising. He helped me to stay balanced and encouraged me to keep moving forward even when I felt stymied for a few days or weeks.

My children and their spouses helped me with editing and some of my technological formatting issues. They were gracious enough to volunteer to take my tests and complete my questionnaires. They helped give me clarity and practical ideas to help me communicate more effectively.

All the illustrations in this book are done by family members. Even my grandchildren worked diligently to draw pictures of the six animals in *The Zoo of You*. I couldn't include every drawing sample, but I appreciate the efforts of every one of them.

Above all, I thank God for taking care of me and helping me to make the transition to retirement. He gave me *The Zoo of You*—a tool I can use for the rest of my life. I pray that it will also be a gift you can use to help you deal with challenges in your lives.

INTRODUCTION

The purpose of this book is twofold.

1. I want to help myself adjust to retirement, with God as my counselor.
2. I want to show you how your natural defense mechanisms can be transformed into divine life skills.

I was inspired to create a virtual "zoo of you" to help me navigate the challenges in my situation. This book is a collection of animals representing life skills needed to overcome obstacles in our lives. They are born from natural defense mechanisms that we use in times of crisis. Throughout my twenty-eight years of counseling, I have noticed how these defense mechanisms have helped people survive and thrive as they move forward in their lives. My goal is to learn to be proactive with these skills and to use them intentionally, not only as a response to intense trauma. Let me introduce these six animal skills to you.

- *Freeze Rabbit* skill is the force inside you that stops to think before acting.
- *Follow Dog* skill is the tendency to follow the rules, to trust a respected person who's in charge.
- *Bond Kangaroo Joey* skill is the ability to ask for help, to bond with a caregiver or loved one.
- *Nurture Elephant* skill is the drive to care for others through nurture and self-sacrifice.
- *Escape Cat* skill is the choice to run away, to escape pain or danger, to seek self-preservation.
- *Fight Lion* skill is the skill of being assertive, taking charge to protect and defend self and others.

I designed a quick sorter test to help you identify your baseline—your natural defense mechanisms. This test will help you see which skills you have been using more frequently. At the end of this book, you will have the opportunity to take the test again. The anticipated result is that you will utilize more and more of the skills as you learn to choose to use them in your daily life.

Take a few minutes to complete the test that follows. Remember to choose all the responses that apply to your skill set at this time. It's fine to pick both a and b responses if they both apply to you.

THE ZOO OF YOU SKILL QUESTIONNAIRE (BASELINE)

1. Are you more likely to be
   a. attached and connected (Bond Kangaroo Joey)
   b. brave and outspoken (Fight Lion)

2. Do you see yourself as
   a. a nurturing caregiver (Nurture Elephant)
   b. a proactive leader (Fight Lion)

3. Are you more
   a. loyal and reliable (Follow Dog)
   b. calm and patient (Freeze Rabbit)

4. Are you more
   a. independent and self-aware (Escape Cat)
   b. bonded to one special person (Bond Kangaroo Joey)

5. Are you more likely to be
   a. bold and decisive (Fight Lion)
   b. non-assertive and trusting (Bond Kangaroo Joey)

6. Are you more likely to be
   a. steady and dependable (Follow Dog)
   b. protective and comforting (Nurture Elephant)

7. Are you more likely to
   a. ask for help (Bond Kangaroo Joey)
   b. freeze in a crisis (Freeze Rabbit)

8. Are you more likely to be
   a. a helpful teacher (Nurture Elephant))
   b. a creative daydreamer (Escape Cat)

9. Are you more likely to be
    a. reflective and observant (Freeze Rabbit)
    b. hard-working and compliant (Follow Dog)

10. Are you more likely to be
    a. determined and focused (Fight Lion)
    b. consistent and trustworthy (Follow Dog)

11. Are you more likely to
    a. go on a vacation to de-stress (Escape Cat)
    b. work first/play later (Nurture Elephant)

12. Would you rather be
    a. invisible (Freeze Rabbit)
    b. in the spotlight (Escape Cat)

Count how many answers you chose for each animal prototype.

Freeze Rabbit _____Bond Kangaroo Joey _____Escape Cat _____
Follow Dog _____Nurture Elephant _____Fight Lion _____

When I took the baseline skill questionnaire, I scored a 4 in the freeze rabbit, follow dog, and nurture elephant categories, 3 in the bond kangaroo joey category, 1 in the escape cat category, and 0 in the fight lion category. It is obvious to me that I could benefit from more skills in the escape cat and fight lion categories, and I need to maintain balance in the other four categories.

Throughout my life, I have learned to think before acting (Freeze Rabbit), follow rules (Follow Dog), care for others (Nurture Elephant), and trust the bond I have with people I love (Bond Kangaroo Joey). I need to learn skills which will help me relax and care for myself, to take life less seriously, and learn to have fun (Escape Cat). I need to learn to assert myself and be brave and courageous (Fight Lion).

CHAPTER 1

THE "ZOO OF YOU" DEFINED

We have all used emotional crutches in our lives. These crutches are natural extensions of the defense mechanisms innate to all of us. They help us get through a hard time, and then we throw them in the closet and forget about them. My goal is to transform these crutches into coping mechanisms we can walk with every day of our lives. I see them personified as animals who can walk us through our crises—a virtual zoo of resources to aid our healing, no longer crutches that get used for a little while and then discarded; this team of animal resources can accompany us through every day and every crisis. Defense mechanisms are no longer temporary crutches. They can become permanent life skills when we learn to use them intentionally.

You have already been introduced to this "zoo." As you will recall, the animals in this zoo are Freeze Rabbit, Follow Dog, Bond Kangaroo Joey, Nurture Elephant, Escape Cat, and Fight Lion. Now I want you to understand how I came up with this idea. Conventionally, the autonomic nervous system uses survival skills (crutches) to get us through crises. Our bodies react to a crisis by springing into action through the sympathetic nervous system, building to a plateau of tension, and then resolving through the parasympathetic nervous system of rest and recovery. The sympathetic nervous system acts as an accelerator, whereas the parasympathetic nervous system puts on the brakes. I began with the familiar concepts of *fight*, *flight*, and *freeze*. Then I thought about my own responses, and the responses I have seen in my clients for twenty-eight years. I realized that sympathetic and parasympathetic responses don't always follow each other. It isn't a smooth transition for most people. It's a stop, start, twist-and-turn kind of ride that shakes you up emotionally like a roller coaster. My personal research netted six different responses, not just three. I identified them as freeze, follow, bond, nurture, escape, and fight. I decided to present them as animals to personify the action of the response more clearly. Consequently, freeze is a rabbit, follow is a dog, bond is a kangaroo joey, nurture is an elephant, escape is a cat, and fight is a lion.

It is my premise that we can learn to utilize the strengths of these animal responses. Then we can make a cognitive choice to use them as skills, at our bidding, not only as a subconscious response. We all have favorite animals and responses that come to us more naturally. However, this is a quest to broaden our animal compatibility, to utilize all the skills in the "zoo of you," not just a few pet animals.

1

I have designed a chart to help you see that each of these animal skills can be divided into skill sets, emphasizing some of the best qualities of each animal skill. Read the four statements referring to each animal skill and mark the ones you think you are already using. You may notice that you have more responses in some categories than others. I have written a chapter on each animal skill set, so you can fine-tune your skills in each category. If you have few skills in a category, you will want to spend more time focusing on the activities which will help you develop those skills that don't seem as natural to you. Take a few moments to mark your responses.

Animal Skill Set Chart

Each of the six animal skills has four statements associated with it. Mark the statements that currently describe you. There is no limit to how many you can select in each row. Then see which statements are not marked. These are the areas you will need to work on the most. This will broaden your response range and help you become a more balanced person.

Freeze Rabbit	R1 I know when to stop and admit powerlessness.	R2 I am usually patient and comfortable waiting for answers.	R3 I am good at watching, observing what's going on around me.	R4 I have learned to be mindful and reflective.
Follow Dog	D1 I am comfortable following a leader.	D2 I am a good listener who pays attention to details.	D3 I am dependable and tend to finish what I start.	D4 I'm a team player who complements others.
Bond Kangaroo Joey	KJ1 I am comfortable asking for help.	KJ2 I believe that being vulnerable is a good thing.	KJ3 I value being connected/ attached in relationships.	KJ4 I find it natural to express gratitude.
Nurture Elephant	E1 My first impulse is to care for others.	E2 I am good at teaching and nurturing.	E3 I am generous with my time, ideas, and possessions.	E4 I am a natural advocate for other people.

Escape Cat	C1 I know when I need to escape/ to get away.	C2 I am good at self-soothing and self-care	C3 I am creative and have hobbies.	C4 I am a visionary who can see the best in a situation.
Fight Lion	L1 I react quickly in a crisis.	L2 I am brave and know when to take risks.	L3 I am not afraid of what others think of me.	L4 I am a decisive leader who doesn't give up.

Animal Skill Set Chart: My Responses

Each of the six animal skills has four statements associated with it. Mark the statements that currently describe you. There is no limit to how many you can choose in each row. Then see which statements are not marked. These are the areas you will need to work on the most. This will broaden your response range and help you become a more balanced person.

Freeze Rabbit	**R1** **I know when to stop and admit powerlessness.**	**R2** **I am usually patient and comfortable waiting for answers.**	R3 I am good at watching, observing what's going on around me.	**R4** **I have learned to be mindful and reflective.**
Follow Dog	**D1** **I am comfortable following a leader.**	**D2** **I am a good listener who pays attention to details.**	**D3** **I am dependable and tend to finish what I start.**	D4 I'm a team player who complements others.
Bond Kangaroo Joey	KJ1 I am comfortable asking for help.	**KJ2** **I believe that being vulnerable is a good thing.**	**KJ3** **I value being connected/ attached in relationships.**	**KJ4** **I find it natural to express gratitude.**
Nurture Elephant	**E1** **My first impulse is to care for others.**	**E2** **I am good at teaching and nurturing.**	E3 I am generous with my time, ideas, and possessions.	**E4** **I am a natural advocate for other people.**

Escape Cat	C1 I know when I need to escape/ to get away.	C2 I am good at self-soothing and self-care	**C3** **I am creative and have hobbies.**	**C4** **I am a visionary who can see the best in a situation.**
Fight Lion	L1 I react quickly in a crisis.	L2 I am brave and know when to take risks.	L3 I am not afraid of what others think of me.	L4 I am a decisive leader who doesn't give up.

Take note of your responses and think about the skill sets you want to develop as you read and reflect on the following chapters. Freeze Rabbit is first followed by Follow Dog, Bond Kangaroo Joey, Nurture Elephant, Escape Cat, and Fight Lion. For each numbered statement, there is a corresponding activity to help you focus on that specific skill in the animal skill set.

Freeze Rabbit (Drawn by Leslie Kirkes)

CHAPTER 2

....

FREEZE RABBIT, LOOKING BACK

Be still and know that I am God.

—Psalm 46:10 ESV

Freeze Rabbit represents the moment you stop in your tracks and feel powerless. This rabbit is a terrified rabbit, frozen in fear, paralyzed, and pasted into the camouflage of background cover. This rabbit experiences tonic immobility and "plays dead" without a voluntary response. Panic comes to mind. Powerlessness quickly follows. Not thinking, not choosing, just stuck, frozen in a state of physical and emotional paralysis.

There is an advantage to being temporarily stuck, however. It forces us to be safe without pursuing safety. It demands a stillness from striving and overanalyzing—a powerful reset of all functions. When you feel the impulse to freeze, picture Freeze Rabbit in your mind.

Looking Back
Examples of My Freeze Rabbit Moments

I selected three out of four rabbit qualities on the animal skill set chart indicating that I have a strong "rabbit freeze" pattern in my life. I looked back and found many examples of my tendency to freeze and reflect before moving on. This is a good quality when used with discretion and not as a paralyzing crutch.

Birth

Birth may seem to be an event, not a memory, but humor me for a moment. Even before we are born, we have a sense of being—a body memory awareness that is a permanent part of who we are. Now imagine the shock of being evicted from a warm, cozy cocoon to enter a cold, unpredictable world. Just like Freeze Rabbit, we experience a frozen moment of panic and powerlessness.

This is the "memory" I have created based on facts and feelings stored in my subconscious mind. It was April 12, 1955. It was 3:20 a.m. in a tiny hospital in Reserve, New Mexico. I was shocked to enter a cold and unfamiliar world, so different than the warm, protective environment I had been basking in for the past nine months. I held my breath and froze emotionally then let out a cry—a cry of surrender and agreement that I would begin this journey of survival in a brave new world. Mom comforted my panic, and my life began. That frozen moment of powerlessness followed by a cry of acceptance provided the transition I needed to start the journey of life outside the womb.

When I got caught in a mouse trap

The freeze rabbit response protects us when we experience intense sudden pain. It activates natural endorphins and numbs the pain until we can handle it. It's an icy-hot feeling that shocks the pain and then gradually releases it. The following story has been told to me so many times that I can imagine it clearly. This is how I picture it.

I was less than two years old, half-crawling and half-walking, when I explored my babysitter's house. My curiosity drew me to a strange contraption on the floor, in the crack between two cabinets. I picked it up and touched the metal bar that was stretched across the wooden base. Suddenly, my finger was snapped into the trap, and I felt a lightening flash of pain! My brain doesn't remember, but my body remembers how painful and shocking it was. Apparently, I had the bad habit of playing with mouse traps. My babysitter wanted to teach me a lesson, so she allowed me to experience getting caught. I can imagine feeling shocked and numb with pain and disbelief. It must have been confusing to me for my caregiver to allow me to experience distress. I am eternally grateful to Mom for coming and rescuing me. To this day, I have an aversion to mice and mouse traps. Even though my brain doesn't consciously remember all the details of this experience, the freeze rabbit response made it part of my permanent psyche.

When my baby boy died

The trauma of grief and loss is well-known to Freeze Rabbit. That feeling of powerlessness, shock, and denial demands an emotional and spiritual reset—a frozen pause before moving forward. I had that kind of experience when my baby boy died.

He was my third child and was born three and a half months early. I had placenta previa and had to be on bed rest. It was driving me crazy to be so inactive. One day, when my mother-in-law came for a visit, I justified taking a break from bed rest for just a little while. I reasoned that I would be okay since she was there to help me. We went shopping for Christmas presents. That was on November 12, 1983. Things went downhill from there, and my baby was born on November 21. He wasn't due until March! He weighed a pound and a half and was only eleven inches long. I never got to hold him in my arms. He was in ICU for thirteen days and then died of necrotizing enterocolitis. I was in shock not only because of the grief and trauma of loss but also because of the tremendous guilt I felt for going shopping that day. I felt like dying myself and know I didn't pay much attention to my two little girls. It was difficult to be happy for Christmas that year. I was frozen in a state of emotional numbness. I had to be still and depend on God to get me through it.

What I learned from that awful experience was that I couldn't take anything for granted anymore. I had to let go of any false guilt and lean on God's grace instead of my own performance. My life perspective changed. Instead of rushing around worrying about daily tasks, I took the time to color pictures with my little girls and leave the dishes in the sink until they went to bed. I learned the value of bonding with them more than directing them. I learned that spending time hanging out together was better than getting all my chores done for the day. It was a huge pause, a dramatic reset in my life. I needed it. It activated my heart and turned off some of my head's overthinking.

When I got in a wreck

This is another example of Freeze Rabbit slamming on the brakes and forcing me to stop and reflect.

It was July 8, 1997. It was a warm, beautiful day, and I was taking my seventeen-year-old daughter for a doctor's appointment. She had been in three car accidents in the past year and a half, and none of them were her fault. She was in a neck brace and was undergoing neurocognitive therapy for head trauma and whiplash. I had a green light as I drove through an intersection. The next thing I knew, there was a crash, and I was frozen in a state of shock and disbelief. On the other side of my green light was a police car running a red light! I had done the most outlandish thing I could imagine! I had crashed into a police car! I have no idea how I got out of the vehicle or what I said to the officer driving the car. He said he had his lights and sirens on, but I did not see the lights or hear the siren. He was going to get rattlesnake venom at the hospital. My daughter was in such shock that she passed out and had to be taken to the hospital in an ambulance. They said there was no additional damage to her physically. I was angry that this had to happen. I was in shock, knowing that I had the green light, and felt vindicated. I had to go to court and was told I was driving carelessly since I was unaware of the officer's emergency approach into the intersection. This freeze rabbit moment traumatized me and made me slow down to look at my life and my priorities. It made me realize I need to be more watchful, attentive, and aware of what's going on around me.

When I had my fifteen-year-old drive in Albuquerque

After that incident, I was afraid to drive. My vehicle was totaled, and I felt paralyzed when I thought about getting in a driver's seat of any kind. Freeze Rabbit still had its grip on me. I knew I had to wait, to be patient, to let myself heal from the trauma before I took the next step forward. However, life goes on, and driving is part of life. The next example shows how I dealt with this feeling of paralysis and fear. It was not courageous, but it was desperate and resourceful.

A few days after the wreck, my seventeen-year-old daughter had an appointment in Albuquerque for neurocognitive therapy. We lived in Alamogordo, three and a half hours away from Albuquerque. This appointment had been scheduled previously since my seventeen-year-old had already been experiencing neurocognitive issues due to her first three wrecks. Now she had an even greater need for therapy, with a fourth wreck to add to the damage. I was paralyzed with fear when I thought about driving in Albuquerque. I thought about canceling the appointment but knew it was critical that we get there somehow. My seventeen-year-old daughter didn't feel comfortable driving in Albuquerque either. In desperation, I asked my fifteen-year-old daughter to drive us. She had her provisional license and was willing to take on the challenge. She was very capable and good at driving, so she did just fine. I know God was watching over us and sent some extra angels to help protect us. I'm appalled to this day that I was frozen in fear and couldn't make myself get in that driver's seat.

Quitting my job at Bethel Baptist Counseling Ministry

How long was Freeze Rabbit going to keep me frozen? It seemed I was driving disabled for the time being.

After that wreck, I was traumatized when I thought of driving. I couldn't imagine driving myself to work. I quit my job at Bethel Baptist Counseling Ministry. I had been working there for three and a half years and had finished the supervision I needed to be a licensed professional counselor. Looking back, I see that it was the right time to make a change. It was that month of transition that forced me to consider a new job—one with a salary that would help pay the bills. By that time, I could drive with caution even though I still didn't make any trips out of town. In August, about six weeks after the wreck, I started working at La Placita Community Residential Facility. Within six months, I got my certification as a licensed professional clinical mental health counselor and became clinical director of the facility. It so happened that I had to drive through the very same intersection where the wreck happened, day after day, to get to my new job. That taught me about desensitization and how it can really make you stronger in time. Freeze Rabbit kept me frozen until I could take positive steps in a new direction of growth and courage.

When my husband had a heart attack

I'm certain Freeze Rabbit made many reappearances, but the one that shocked me back to that place of intense emotional paralysis happened twenty-three years after the wreck of 1997.

On Wednesday, June 17, 2020, my husband had a heart attack. We had been to a church Bible study that evening. We had our own church in Tularosa, New Mexico, where he was the pastor, and I was the music director. It seemed like a normal day, and we were both content with our life. Right before bed, he had chest pain, shortness of breath, felt weak, and was sweating. He insisted that he needed to go to the hospital to get evaluated. I was terrified at the thought that I would have to drive him there. I was even more terrified at the thought that I might lose him, and it would be my fault if I couldn't get him there in time. It was dark, about 10:00 p.m., and I felt a sense of panic since I have a slight degree of night blindness. I felt paralyzed in the moment and thought about calling an ambulance or making my husband drive himself. I prayed and suddenly felt disconnected from myself in a strange state of resolution that drove my fear beneath the surface. My fear was frozen, and I felt a stronger presence taking my place. I drove faster than I usually would have but didn't drive carelessly. I got to the hospital and had trouble finding the ER entrance due to construction. My husband helped me get headed in the right direction, and we took him to the ER. Before we knew it, they had him in a room, and the cardiologist came and put a stent in his heart. They said he would have died if he had waited forty-five more minutes to get to the hospital. Somehow, I was even allowed to go back with him; I slipped through the COVID cracks and was there to welcome him after his surgery. God watched over us and spoke to me through the stillness. That freeze rabbit stillness got me through the storm until I could see the light of the morning after.

Unexpected driving in Oklahoma City

After my husband's heart attack, he realized that living at a lower altitude would help both his heart and his lungs since he had already been diagnosed with pulmonary hypertension. We eventually bought a home in Duncan, Oklahoma, where his medical condition is much better. I was soon to realize that the lower altitude did not eliminate my visits from Freeze Rabbit however.

My husband's glaucoma had been getting worse, so his regular doctor sent him to a specialist in Oklahoma City. It was supposed to be a consultation, so I was not worried. My husband always drives when we go to big cities, so I curled into my comfortable role of reading a book out loud while we traveled. When we arrived for the appointment, my comfort was soon disrupted. Before I knew it, the doctor dilated my husband's eyes and did laser surgery, on the spot! I realized I had to drive home to Duncan, ninety miles away! I proceeded to have a panic attack, compliments of Freeze Rabbit. After the frozen moment of truth where I let myself feel the fear, reality surfaced, and I told my husband he couldn't drive. He said he could, but I knew it wasn't safe for him to drive. I resolved to do what I had to do. So I followed the GPS lady in my phone all the way home. It was scary, but I held my breath and took a few deep breaths and told my husband to close his eyes, and we were just fine! Freeze Rabbit allowed me to have my meltdown and release all the tension so that I could refocus and concentrate on driving safely.

Freeze Rabbit, Looking Back, Your Turn

I can think of more Freeze Rabbit moments in my life, but it's time for you to reflect. When have you felt frozen, traumatized, powerless, or stuck? When have you been forced to be patient and wait for answers? When have you stopped to reflect, observe, and practice mindfulness? Write your own memories of past Freeze Rabbit moments in the space that follows.

_____

_____

_____

_____

_____

_____

_____

_____

_____

CHAPTER 3

....

FReeze RABBIT SKILL SeT, LOOKING FORWARD: R1, R2, R3, R4

Now it's time to look forward. How can we learn to use the "freeze rabbit" resource as a strength? Let's look at each of Freeze Rabbit's characteristics on the animal skill set chart. You may already have this skill, but you can choose to use it more often when it seems appropriate. You may think you lack this skill, but you can develop more proficiency in this area by practicing the following guidelines.

Freeze Rabbit 1
I Know When to Stop and Admit Powerlessness

1. *Stop.* Imagine Freeze Rabbit frozen in contemplation. You may know this as "the deer in the headlights" look. Force yourself to take slow, deep breaths. Count to four on the inhale, hold your breath for the count of four, and slowly count to four on the exhale. (You can count to six or eight if you prefer). Repeat.
2. *Cool down.* Continue deep breathing while you release the intense emotions and acknowledge that you are vulnerable. Give yourself permission to feel inadequate in the moment.
3. *Think.* I am safe. I don't have to be in control. I can't do anything to fix this situation by myself. I need God to take over. I agree that this is good. I will only act when the danger is past.

_____

_____

_____

_____

_____

Stop right now to think about how you are feeling. Is this skill easy for you, or do you feel resistance inside yourself? Write down your thoughts and consider that vulnerability is one of the most difficult emotions to accept. Think about when this skill could help you.

_____
_____
_____
_____
_____

Freeze Rabbit 2
I Am Usually Patient and Comfortable Waiting for Answers

1. *Be still.* Pay attention to your body and make sure you relax all your muscles. Imagine that you are floating, hanging limp, breathing, and waiting.
2. *Remember.* Your brain can't think straight when you are flooded with emotion. You must let the brain fog and emotional smoke settle before you can see clearly to know what move to make.
3. *Wait.* The answer will come. Believe that the best answer is worth waiting for, and wisdom will speak to you through the stillness. Remember that you must wait for Jell-O to be Jell-O. If you don't wait, you just have juice.

_____
_____
_____
_____
_____

Write down your thoughts about these suggestions remembering that this is a skill that can be useful to everyone when used at the appropriate times.

_____
_____
_____
_____
_____

Freeze Rabbit 3
I Am Good at Watching and Observing What Is Going On Around Me

1. *Look.* Notice everything around you without bias, without preconceived expectations. Let your brain take a mental picture of what you see. Note the details that are there without embellishing or minimizing what you see.
2. *Listen.* Be quiet as you truly listen to what is going on around you, whether it is a spoken word or other sounds in nature. Let the sounds reverberate and settle in. Don't think about what you are going to say as soon as the sounds cease. Just let the meaning of the sounds sink into your brain.

3. *Observe.* Look at the big picture. See what is really going on. Don't make assumptions based on what you expect or want. Just be a part of the moment without adding or subtracting from it.

Take time to write how you feel about this concept and how you could grow in this area if awareness is one of your challenges.

Freeze Rabbit 4
I Have Learned to Be Mindful and Reflective

1. *Be present.* Think only about this moment, this situation, this place. Do not think about yesterday or tomorrow. Only now. Only one thought at a time. If another thought tries to distract you, let it slide off the edge of your brain, just like a ball rolling down a slide.
2. *Be balanced.* Be aware of your emotions, but do not immerse yourself in feelings only. Be aware of your cognitive thoughts, but do not restrict yourself to logical reasoning.
3. *Be wise.* Blend the logical thinking and emotional thinking until you can see the truth based on both sides of your brain working in harmony. This is one of the most difficult skills to achieve. Reflect on your thoughts in the space that follows.

CHAPTER 4

....

FINDING THE FREEZE RABBIT BALANCE

We have established that the "freeze rabbit" skill is a good skill to have, for everyone, some of the time but not all the time. How are we to know if we have too much or too little Freeze Rabbit in our lives? Consider the following thoughts to help you figure out where you are on Freeze Rabbit's scale.

The Benefits of Freeze Rabbit

At the center of a trauma or dilemma is the moment when you freeze and realize you're in an uncomfortable, threatening place. It might be very dangerous, a chronic trigger for anxiety, or a crossroads' moment of decision. The first response is often that "stop in your tracks'" feeling when you are stuck in the middle of the swirling chaos of the situation. Freezing is not a bad thing. It can prevent you from acting foolishly and can give you time to think of options. The "ice pack" on an emotional wound can reduce swelling and inflammation by cooling the emotion and giving the logical brain time to thaw out. Realizing your powerlessness can unlock the wisdom of God and let Him work His purpose in you without letting your own striving or overthinking get in the way. Benefits of Freeze Rabbit's skill are learning to be cautious, patient, reflective, observant, and mindful. A calmness can penetrate the frozen stillness and help you to be more observant and mindful, to learn the art of breathing and floating in the moment. Pausing to think can give you time to reboot, reset, and reconsider the choices available to you. It can be a valuable toggle tool—a transition at various junctures in life. It can be a time of rest and renewal—a serene sanctuary where strength can be rebuilt and rejuvenated.

The Handicaps of Freeze Rabbit

On the other hand, Freeze Rabbit has its downside if used too long or too often. If you remain in this frozen state, you may forget to use other skills of survival. You will risk being stuck in a frozen hole of nothingness, sinking deeper into darkness and despair. You may have episodes of panic that don't resolve easily. You may have frozen, dark thoughts that refuse to consider positive solutions.

You may obsess about the negative possibilities and overthink the mistakes you have made. You may be overwhelmed with guilt and forget that there is light outside this frozen ice cube cave.

In this state of frozenness, you may come to believe that you are alone and that everyone is against you.

You may think life is cold and lifeless and has no meaning. You will feel emotionally paralyzed with fear and will be terrified of making mistakes.

Too Much Freeze Rabbit

The worst extreme of Freeze Rabbit is when you let it define you. You always walk with that limp of paralyzed fear. People expect you to be ineffective and unavailable and apathetic and disengaged from life. You make excuses for yourself and remain in this comfortable state of irresponsibility and camouflage of frozen strength. You make no demands on yourself or others. You pretend to be invisible and become immune to anything healthy or relational. You avoid challenges and never take steps toward goals. You become a frozen statue that people walk around. You forget you are a person and begin to believe that your existence is meaningless.

Too Little Freeze Rabbit

So is it an option to throw away Freeze Rabbit's skill and never use it at all? It is an option but not a healthy one. Eliminating transitions altogether invites more chaos and risk, more mistakes, and unnecessary self-created traumas. Freezing preserves energy and crystallizes focus. It gives direction and destination to the action which follows.

A Healthy Freeze Rabbit Balance

The best use of Freeze Rabbit's skill is to use it as a haven of solitude—a place to "touch base" and regroup. It is an anchor which holds you fast and prevents drifting. It encourages you to reflect on your next move, to strengthen your inner self, and find a true spiritual center. This is the essential inner balance that keeps you functioning. It's like the circadian rhythm of sleep. There is an optimum amount of sleep and/or rest that you need each day, every day. This is the rejuvenation and restoration that you need. A freeze too deep can keep you from growing, but no freeze at all can make your life spin out of control.

To rate yourself in the freeze rabbit skill set, you may consider the following questions:

1. In the morning, do you wake up feeling rested and ready for the day?
    If your answer is yes, give yourself five points.
    If your answer is no, too little sleep, give yourself six points.
    If your answer is no, too much sleep, give yourself four points.
    Your answer: _____

2. Do you often feel sluggish? Do you have difficulty making decisions?

    If your answer is yes to both questions, give yourself three points.

    If your answer is yes to one question, give yourself four points.

    If your answer is no to both questions, give yourself five points.

    Your answer: _____

3. Do you rush from one thing to another? Do you have trouble focusing on one thing?

    If your answer is yes to both questions, give yourself seven points.

    If your answer is yes to one question, give yourself six points.

    If your answer is no to both questions, give yourself five points.

    Your answer: _____

4. Are you stuck in a boring routine? Are you afraid to try new things?

    If your answer is yes to both questions, give yourself three points.

    If your answer is yes to one question, give yourself four points.

    If your answer is no to both questions, give yourself five points.

    Your answer: _____

5. Do you stay busy doing many things? Do you lack a sense of purpose or direction?

    If your answer is yes to both questions, give yourself seven points.

    If your answer is yes to one question, give yourself six points.

    If your answer is no to both questions, give yourself five points.

    Your answer: _____

6. Do you have a time each day when you intentionally pause and reflect on your day?

    If your answer is yes, give yourself five points.

    If your answer is no, I don't have time to stop, give yourself six points.

    If your answer is no, my life is always on pause, give yourself four points.

    Your answer: _____

7. Do you like who you are? Do you feel grounded and secure in your life situation? Are you aware of strengths and weaknesses in yourself but accept and love yourself anyway?

    If your answer is yes to all three questions, give yourself five points.

    If you feel extra-confident in your ability to answer yes, give yourself six points.

    If you feel slightly less than confident in your ability to answer yes, give yourself four points.

    Your answer: _____

Your overall freeze rabbit score

1._____2. _____ 3. _____ 4. _____5. _____ 6. _____ 7. _____
_____Total divided by seven =_____

Conclusion/Summary/Recommendations

If your average score is five, congratulations, you are a super freeze rabbit!

If your average score is less than five, you may need to urge that rabbit to get moving.

Suggestions: Try a new hobby. Go to the gym and/or do cardio exercise. Make a slight change to your routine.
Bottom line: Pick an activity that will warm you up and get you out of your comfort zone.

If your average score is more than five, you may need to slow down that rabbit.

Suggestions: Try meditation. Sit and watch a sunset. Walk a mile on a treadmill.
Bottom line: Pick an activity that will cool you down and help you to relax.

Follow Dog (Drawn by Dan Abercrombie)

CHAPTER 5

....

FOLLOW DOG, LOOKING BACK

Whatever you do, work heartily, as for the Lord and not for men, knowing that from the Lord you will receive the inheritance as your reward. You are serving the Lord Christ.
—*Colossians 3:23–24 ESV*

Follow Dog Skill

The "follow dog" picture is represented by our own dog, Bob, as drawn by my husband. My husband is the mentor, and Bob is the perfect follower. Bob is the epitome of the skill I am presenting. He wakes up every morning with the desire to please his master and is truly "man's best friend." He follows and learns and remains consistently loyal. He is always ready to go the extra mile, literally. He rarely needs a leash because his heart is tied to my husband's will and word.

The follow dog skill represents the impulse to follow and learn from others, to trust a strong leader as a mentor and authority. This dog always comes home, always shows devotion and obedience and trust. This response looks for direction and resources outside self and rarely questions or resists leadership. This is a very good quality but can become a constraint when it defines you. Following someone's lead, striving for harmony, and pleasing people may be a good choice but can sometimes feel like a leash—a bungee cord pulling a person back from moving forward. It's important to know who you are following and where you want to go. It's never a good choice to follow blindly. When you feel the impulse to follow, picture Follow Dog in your mind.

Looking Back
Examples of My Follow Dog Moments

With three out of four Follow Dog qualities on the animal skill set chart, I should be a pretty good follower. My new epiphany is that I need to trust the brain and heart and soul God gave me. Following His truth is first. Following others can be good, but it can't take the place of following your own heart.

Following in Mom's footsteps

Ever since I can remember, I have looked up to my mother and have admired her strength and determination. She was a woman ahead of her time that followed her dream all the way from Maine to New Mexico. She had just graduated from nurse's training and wanted to travel all the way to Reserve, New Mexico, to work in a tiny hospital there. Her parents wouldn't let her go alone, so she convinced her nursing friend to go with her. They both got jobs in the little country hospital and were both married within three months! My mother was a working mother in the 1950s, long before it was popular for women to have successful careers.

My mother's standards are high, for herself and others. She inspired me to work hard and aspire to reach my full potential. Following rules and fulfilling obligations was standard procedure. She encouraged me to finish my college education before I got married so I would have my own career as well. It gave me a sense of significance to know I was following in Mom's footsteps and getting her approval.

You can't win them all

At school, I excelled academically and was often told so. My goal was to please my teachers and get good grades. In my writing classes, it was the most evident. I wrote what my teachers expected and soon learned to follow the preferred writing style of each one. In high school, I wrote long flowery essays but found that shorter, more concise documentaries got me better grades in college. My self-worth was wrapped up in my ability to please teachers and to be recognized for it. One teacher in my sophomore year of high school taught me a more valuable life lesson. I could not get the brain out whole when I was trying to dissect a star fish. This favorite teacher taught me that "you can't win them all." I've had to learn this lesson repeatedly. He taught me to follow my natural aptitudes, not to work so hard at my unnatural ones. Follow Dog would explain it this way: If you're a collie, be the best collie you can be. Don't try to be a Great Dane or any other kind of dog. Be your best self and follow your own propensities.

Side by side, not follow

Marriage was a totally new type of relationship for me. I was accustomed to pleasing parents, teachers, and supervisors. Now I was in a one-on-one relationship with someone who loved me for myself, with no need to be perfect. My follow dog people-pleasing pattern kicked in and caused me some unnecessary disappointment with myself. My husband is my opposite, so following him didn't work well for either one of us. My thinking is "upside down" from his. My first impulse was to try to figure out what he wanted and then please him by doing it. To my surprise, that didn't work as well as it did on my teachers. First, I couldn't read his mind, and I couldn't predict when he might change his mind. I tried to change myself into a copy of him, and then I realized I was losing myself. That wasn't a good choice because he fell in love with who I really was, not a puppet of himself. I realized that real love was walking side by side, not following.

Follow the leader?

When my oldest daughter was three years old, I realized that she was the one making decisions for me. She was taking charge of her younger sister and helping me so much that I forgot I was the one in charge. I realized that I needed to be the parent. That meant my goal and my role needed to be adjusted. I had to get out of the following role and be a leader, a teacher, even a disciplinarian, at times. That was a real challenge for me. I didn't want to be the "bad guy" when it came to discipline, so I invariably leaned on my husband to handle reprimands. Now I realize that was unfair because I painted an unrealistic picture in my children's minds. I had to learn to be a parent-leader so my children could build security through following me.

Fishing foibles

My husband taught me how to bait my own hook, how to cast it, and how to get the fish off the hook. However, I still don't fish like he fishes. I can only handle one pole at a time, and I often get it caught in the rocks and bushes. I am diligent about watching my line but often lack the technique to land the fish successfully. Following got me started; practice will get me more fish. Since I need to practice a lot, we go fishing a lot. That pleases both of us.

Walking in the dark

Hunting with my husband is all about following. Before the break of dawn, I follow him step-by-step, through the darkness, as we make our way to our deer blind. It is my fear that I will be lost if I lose sight of his back or miss even one step. When we get to the blind, I follow his sign language and try to make no sound as we enter. This proves to be impossible since one of us invariably bumps the side of the blind. Next, we sit and watch, being careful not to make any jerky movements. This hunting season, I counted thirty trips to the blind before we got a deer. Then all the following was worth it!

Follow Dog, Looking Back, Your Turn

I have many more examples of Follow Dog in my life, but it's time for you to think of your own examples. Use the following space to write your own memories.

_____

_____

_____

_____

_____

_____

_____

CHAPTER 6

....

FOLLOW DOG SKILL SET, LOOKING FORWARD: D1, D2, D3, D4

You may be a natural leader and find it difficult to follow. On the other hand, you may tend to follow and resist the role of leader. Let's look at each Follow Dog characteristic from the animal skill set chart. Learning the skills associated with Follow Dog is beneficial whether you use them often or just occasionally.

Dog 1
I Am Comfortable Following a Leader

1. *Think.* I don't always have to be in charge. I don't know everything there is to know. I might learn something new.
2. *Trust.* Ascertain that your leader is trustworthy, and then surrender to the idea of following. It's important to trust others or you will always be lonely and isolated.
3. *Respect.* Maybe you know more than the leader, but it's still okay to follow. Learning to follow a chain of command is an important life skill.

_____

_____

_____

_____

_____

Take a few moments to write down how you are feeling about this advice. Which parts are easy, and which guidelines are more difficult?

_____

_____

_____

_____

Dog 2
I Am a Good Listener Who Pays Attention to Details

1. *Listen.* Really listen, not just hear the words as sounds. Value the person who is speaking. Take the time to care about that person's opinions and ideas.
2. *Pay attention.* Focus on what is being said. Train your brain not to wander. Picture a compass in your mind and force yourself to keep your thoughts pointed north, not any other direction. The context and the meaning of the conversation are vitally important. Don't just wait for a break in the conversation so you can insert your own ideas.
3. *Details.* Make sure you can remember at least three details you can mention when it's your turn to speak. That will help you to connect with the person and ensure that you understand what they are saying.

_____

_____

_____

_____

_____

Write down your thoughts and challenges here.

_____

_____

_____

_____

Dog 3
I Am Dependable and Tend to Finish What I Started

1. *Remember.* Even small tasks are important. Someone is counting on you to do your part. Consistency in small things builds character and helps you be a loyal friend and worker.
2. *Finish what you started because it builds a sense of purpose and accomplishment.* It gives you closure to get things done.
3. *Don't give up easily.* Even when the task is difficult, keep trying. Tenacity gives you courage and builds faith and confidence.

_____

_____

_____

_____

Record your thoughts on the following lines.

_____

_____

_____

_____

_____

Dog 4
I'm a Team Player Who Complements Others

1. *Think.* Together is better. Alone is lonely. We can get more done as a team. Teams are organized, and I can learn my role and do it well.
2. *Teams have coaches.* I am not the coach. My job is to do what I'm told. This is good. Submitting to authority and following rules is necessary in society.
3. *Remember.* My small part is important. It fits in with all the other small roles and makes a better whole. I can learn to enjoy being a part of a bigger whole, not to call attention to myself or others, but to complement others.

_____

_____

_____

_____

_____

Write down your thoughts about being a team player.

_____

_____

_____

_____

CHAPTER 7

FINDING THE FOLLOW DOG BALANCE

There are benefits to both following and leading. Let's explore the benefits of both and find where you are on the "follow dog" scale.

The Benefits of Follow Dog

Following is one of the best ways to learn skills. Before you came to the realization of self, you needed parents and guardians to stabilize and secure your growth process. In a similar way, having a trustworthy mentor and choosing to follow in his/her footsteps can be a very good choice. Pacing, walking, repeating, and following can help you learn the value of consistency. You will develop trust through harmony as you traverse a path with someone leading you as a companion and guide. Follow Dog is a skill that can teach wisdom and discernment as you gain knowledge and understanding. It can help you to surrender your need to be right or in control. It can strengthen relationships as you listen and consider another person's opinion. It can help you learn empathy and sensitivity to the needs of another person. You learn the discipline of obedience and the value of loyalty. You can become reliable and trustworthy as you consistently follow the pattern set by someone who has your best interest in mind. The most important factor in this equation is discernment, so it's imperative that you find someone who is worthy of being followed. Then the follow dog skill is enhanced, not manipulated.

The Handicaps of Follow Dog

Following blindly can lead you to a place of lostness—a place where you have no idea who you are and no idea where you are going. Following is good when you are learning skills and need to practice them under supervision, but there is a point where you will need to find your own path. You will always need someone to consult and encourage you, but to follow incessantly can cripple your own progress. You may rely on your mentor's judgment and forget to think for yourself. You may slide into a servant role and do things out of compulsion rather than purpose. You may become bored with repetition and lose your sense of wonder or creativity. You may feel used and devalued and taken for granted. You may struggle with boundary issues, unable to determine whether you should say yes or say no.

Too Much Follow Dog

When you follow too much, you become a people pleaser—someone who has no personal significance other than pleasing the mentor. You become Follow Dog—the one who always pleases your master and has no choices of your own. You may be a perfectionist and a very hard worker who loses sight of the goal. You may become rigid and obsessive in your thinking. You don't take responsibility for making decisions because you never have to set your own precedence or choose any of your own directions. It is easy to settle for this type of existence because you are always cared for as long as you keep following. It is easy to slip into the victim role and blame the leader for anything that goes wrong. There is a strange kind of power that comes from following. You have the power to go along for the ride and never bear the consequence of making wrong choices. It is almost as if you are a robot who acts the part but never lives it. It is a huge sacrifice to make but feels safe and secure if you are only conditioned to follow.

Too Little Follow Dog

To eliminate the follow dog skill completely is to let your pride run free, to think you are the captain of your universe. There is great danger in this because you are likely to trip over your own feet while your head is in the clouds. It is necessary to keep the perspective of Follow Dog, or you will never know how to see yourself accurately in relation to others. If you are always ahead of others, or above others, you will never learn to respect others or value their ideas. You will walk alone on an unmarked path and have no one to help you up when you fall.

A Healthy Follow Dog Balance

Yes, you need the follow dog skill, but you also need to know when to stop following. That might mean you will be alone for a time, lead someone else, and eventually find a new person to follow. Cross-training, switching places, and maintaining resilience will help you use the follow dog skill wisely.

The following questions will help you find where you are on the follow dog continuum and figure out what needs to be adjusted.

1. Do you have someone in your life that you trust when you need advice or encouragement?
   If your answer is yes, give yourself five points.
   If your answer is no, I can handle things on my own, give yourself six points.
   If your answer is no, I have too many people telling me what to do, give
   yourself four points. Your answer: _____

2. Do you feel bored with your daily routine, as if you're going around in circles?

    If your answer is no, give yourself five points.

    If your answer is yes, I'm afraid to change my routine, give yourself four points.

    If your answer is yes, I have trouble deciding what option to choose, give yourself six points.

    Your answer: _____

3. Do you feel as if you're winning a race, but there's no one there to celebrate with you?

    If your answer is no, give yourself five points.

    If your answer is yes, I'd rather celebrate myself, give yourself six points.

    If your answer is yes, I think my friends have abandoned me, give yourself 4 points.

    Your answer: _____

4. Do you find it hard to make decisions on your own?

    If your answer is no, give yourself five points.

    If your answer is yes, but I don't trust anyone to advise me, give yourself six points.

    If your answer is yes, I know I will disappoint someone no matter what I choose, give yourself four points.

    Your answer: _____

5. Do you enjoy being a member of a team?

    If your answer is yes, give yourself five points.

    If your answer is no, I prefer to do things on my own, give yourself six points.

    If your answer is no, I feel too much pressure to please everyone, give yourself four points.

    Your answer: _____

6. Do you enjoy hanging out with someone who respects you? Do you maintain the relationship even when the person doesn't agree with you?

    If you can say yes to both questions, give yourself five points.

    If you like the respect but can't handle the disagreement, give yourself four points.

    If you enjoy a good argument and don't care if you are respected, give yourself six points.

    Your answer: _____

7. Do you trust yourself as much as you trust your friends? Can you accept constructive criticism?

    If you can say yes to both questions, give yourself five points.

    If you say no to the second question, give yourself six points.

    If you say no to the first question, give yourself four points.

    Your answer: _____

Your overall follow dog score

Tally up your answers from all seven questions. Then average them by dividing your total score by seven.

1. ____ 2. _____ 3. _____ 4. _____ 5. _____ 6. _____ 7. _____
_____Total divided by seven =_____

Conclusion/Summary/Recommendations

Follow Dog

If your average score is 5, congratulations, you are a super Follow Dog!

If your average score is less than 5, you may tend to follow too much.

Suggestions: Go on a trip by yourself. Buy something without consulting someone else. Volunteer to lead a group activity.
Bottom line: Do something that gets your follow dog to step out, to make an independent decision. Challenge yourself to be a leader, not a follower, sometimes.

If your average score is more than 5, you may have the idea that you must always be in control.

Suggestions: Join a team or group where you're not the leader/facilitator. Learn to say, "You may be right." Force yourself to ride in the back seat.
Bottom line: Do something that teaches your follow dog to step back. Teach him that he doesn't always have to be "top dog." Learn to follow a leader and follow rules.

Bond Kangaroo Joey (Drawn by Amber Weeks)

CHAPTER 8

....

BOND KANGAROO JOEY, LOOKING BACK

For You formed my inward parts; You knitted me together in my mother's womb. I praise You for I am fearfully and wonderfully made. Wonderful are Your works; my soul knows it very well. My frame was not hidden from You, when I was being made in secret, intricately woven in the depths of the earth.
—Psalm 139:13–15 ESV

Bond Kangaroo Joey Skill

The bond kangaroo joey skill represents the need for connection, the impulse to cry out for help and attach to a person we love and trust. Kangaroo Joeys are totally dependent on their mothers and seek connection and protection through cohesive bonding. One month after gestation, a joey is approximately an inch long and crawls into its mother's pouch for the remaining four to fifteen months of development. This is the most vulnerable position I can imagine: needing sustenance and connection, crying out for help with no means of self-support or volition. Being in this cocoon of protection can be a blissful, comfortable place to "hang out" and develop without having to worry about responsibilities and dangers. This forced vulnerability and helplessness demands dependence. It is a bond that is undeniably necessary and useful. Learning to ask for help and choosing to be vulnerable can be a gift and a learned asset. On the other hand, choosing to stay stuck in a dependent role can be paralyzing and suffocating, a loss of self, a dormancy of development. When you feel the impulse to bond, picture Bond Kangaroo Joey in your mind.

Looking Back
Examples of My Bond Kangaroo Joey Moments

My scores showed three out of four Kangaroo Joey responses on the animal skill set chart. Here are some of my bond kangaroo Joey memories.

And then there were three

Brand-new babies are the epitome of Bond Kangaroo Joeys. Being totally dependent, they have no choice but to depend on parents for all their sustenance. Asking for help through crying and fretting is the only option. All babies are vulnerable and have the need to attach. When they receive the love and attention they need, they learn that it is safe to attach to other people in secure ways. Bonding as an infant results in secure attachment. This builds a strong foundation for healthy relationships in the future.

After my first cry of life, I was cuddled and swaddled and cherished by my parents. They had been married almost a year, and I was the gift they had been waiting for. My mother was a nurse who came from Maine to work in the tiny Catron County Hospital in Reserve, New Mexico. Dad was a rancher and had a job delivering the mail each day. I was the first of five children. My mother stayed home with me until she started a new job as a public health nurse. I was cherished by both parents and got all the attention I needed.

Babysitter bonds

As a natural Kangaroo Joey, I can imagine wishing Mom could stay home with me forever. That wasn't possible, so Mom found me my first babysitter. As I have been told, she adored me and took very good care of me. I don't remember too many details about her but know she died of breast cancer unexpectedly shortly after my third birthday. Her daughter took care of me after that but got married and moved away. This babysitter taught me to love singing. I remember hearing her sing, "Que Sera, Sera, Whatever Will Be, Will Be." From her, I learned that music builds a bond of love and connection. My third babysitter was the one I grew most attached to, especially since she had a daughter close to my age. This babysitter took her time to include me in everything she was doing. I remember helping her pick pepinos (cucumbers) in the garden. I remember that she taught me how to eat liver with less complaining. She put fried potatoes and liver in a tortilla and rolled them up like a burrito. She had a way of soothing unpleasant feelings and made me feel secure. I thought of her as a second mother. One day, I got in trouble for not wanting to go home when Mom came to pick me up. At my babysitter's house, I could be that kangaroo Joey without a care in the world. Things were relaxed, and I didn't have to worry about growing up.

Keep a song in your heart

My Kangaroo Joey heart longed for more attachment. I wanted to know I was loved and protected and cherished. Dad didn't talk much, so he showed me his love in a different way. One day, when I was about five years old, he asked me to sing with him. He taught me a little song by Gene Autry: "If You'll Let Me Be Your Little Sweetheart." I still sing that song to this day and have sung it to my four kids and eight grandkids. Singing that song with Dad started a legacy of love through music. I realized that singing was a way to be vulnerable and open in a way that was difficult for me. The melody seemed to carry the meaning in a different way than lyrics alone. Through the years, I have realized that I am a lot like Dad. I feel more comfortable sending out lyrics of love than hugs and kisses.

Dad doesn't just sing songs; he composes songs of his own. Every song he ever wrote comes straight from his heart and expresses an overflow of love. Here's an example of his love for me when he worried about my safety. I was eighteen years old and was returning home from college for the first time. It was December, and I was flying home for Christmas. I was flying from Asheville, North Carolina, to Albuquerque, New Mexico, changing planes in Dallas. My flight from Dallas to Albuquerque was delayed. Dad made up a song about me as he and Mom anxiously waited for me to arrive. It was in the middle of the night with no cell phones, and they had no idea if I was going to make it home. He put his worries and fears into a prayer song for me to be safe on that stormy night. When I got off that plane, I felt all the love he had put into that song. The kangaroo Joey bond was still strong.

Even now, I look forward to singing with him every time I return to visit. Now our favorite song to sing is, "Daddy Sang Bass." The circle won't be broken as long as we keep a song in our hearts.

Quality time with Mom

Mom and I have always had a bond that connects us through work and shared activities. Since Mom was at work every weekday, we spent time bonding by washing dishes together and sharing thoughts of the day every evening. We did a lot of philosophizing and dreaming when we stood side by side sharing thoughts and stories. It was a connection that grew as we spent more and more quality time together. That's why I still prefer washing dishes by hand and only use the dishwasher when someone else initiates it.

On weekends, Mom and I would clean the house together. Work always came before play, but after the work was done, we would play boardgames. Now when I go home to visit, playing Rummikub and Phase 10 with Mom are some of my favorite pastimes.

Mom and I also have walking in common. Staying active, pacing, and pondering have become therapeutic for me, probably because that's what Mom has modeled for me. Walking our "ten thousand steps a day" is much sweeter when walking and talking together.

Marriage bond

I had always longed for that connection, that bond that I could trust to last forever. College was over, so now my heart was ready for marriage. I missed New Mexico, so I applied for jobs as an elementary school teacher all over the state. The job I secured was in Lordsburg, New Mexico, as a second grade teacher. For five months, I bonded with second graders, but where was my future husband?

It was January 1978, and my wish was about to be granted. It was raining, and I noticed a guy moving into the apartment across from mine. His mother was helping him move in. I did a very uncharacteristic thing for me. I invited them in for cookies and spiced tea. I could see the bond he had with his mother and was impressed that he showed her so much respect. He had a job with the

Soil Conservation Service and had been tipped off by someone in Reserve (my hometown) that I was a nice girl in Lordsburg he should find. He found me, and I found him. I was struck by his authenticity, his strength of character, and his dry humor. I felt I could be vulnerable and that he would always be strong and protective. A year and a half later, we were married.

After two years of teaching in Lordsburg, New Mexico, I was now a married woman. My husband's job moved us all over New Mexico. I was content to leave teaching behind and looked forward to being a mother. First, we moved to Santa Rosa, New Mexico, where we had our first child, and I completed my master's degree in counseling. Then we moved to Mountainair, New Mexico, where we had our second child. We wanted a place out in the country, so we bought a farm in Willard, New Mexico, and planted pinto beans. The next event happened when we lived in Willard.

Asking for help when I was on bed rest

Bonding is not the sole attribute of a kangaroo Joey. Asking for help is a necessary part of the package. Imagine being carried in a pouch all day without any way to take care of yourself.

I was forced to acknowledge that involuntary helplessness when I was on bed rest before the birth of our third child. I made quilts, crocheted afghans, read books, and did my best to care for my two little girls. My husband still had to go to work every day. Two ladies from church came to clean my house once a week. My two toddlers were running around trying to help me, but I was greatly restricted in what I could do. I had to accept help and realized this was the beginning of a special bond with these ladies. Another friend went with me to doctor's appointments and helped me care for my two toddlers. To my dismay, my baby was born three and a half months early. (I have already told you the story of my guilty feelings about getting off bed rest one day.) These three ladies helped me find comfort when I was grieving the loss of my baby. They helped me in ways I didn't even have the strength or will to ask for. It was then that I felt carried because I had no power to carry myself.

My husband's next job was in Alamogordo, New Mexico. By then, we had two more children, and our family was complete: three daughters and one son on this earth and one son in heaven. First, we lived in a trailer park in Alamogordo, then we moved south of town and planted a pistachio orchard. Finally, we bought a farm in Tularosa, New Mexico, just thirteen miles north of Alamogordo.

Rescued from "drowning"

On that farm in Tularosa, we had cows, goats, irrigated pasture, and a reservoir where we stored the water for irrigating. One summer, my husband and kids all wanted to go swimming in our reservoir. They wanted me to join them. My swimming experience was very limited, but I reluctantly agreed to get in the water. I took a few cautious steps, and before I knew it, the water was over my head. I cried out for help and climbed up on top of my husband's head. In my terrifying grip of fear, I clung to him as he sank like a rock down into the mud. I had pulled him down into the mud and wouldn't let go. I'm so thankful that he managed to walk out with me on top of his head. That was a "cry for help" that he will never forget, nor will I. My kangaroo joey instinct depended totally on him to save me. I felt helpless, vulnerable, and powerless to help myself.

Seeking my own counseling

After fifteen years as a stay-at-home mom, I began my counseling career. I was thirty-nine years old and asked myself if I was too old for a new beginning. It didn't take long for me to realize I had a lot of issues I needed help with. The more I counseled people, the more I realized I was codependent and insecure in my own life. It was difficult to transition from being a stay-at-home mom to a working woman. I knew I needed counseling myself, but I was too embarrassed to see a counselor in Alamogordo where everyone might know me. So I went to see a Christian counselor in Roswell two hours away. He helped me to understand that I needed to look up to God for my strength, not to my husband or other people in my life. As I learned to ground myself in God's truth, I began to reach out to others in a healthier way. Asking for help taught me how to be a better person and a better counselor.

Accepting help detangling my crochet yarn

Now that I am retired, I have begun to crochet again. Along with the joy and challenge of creativity, I realize the frustration of tangled yarn. On one occasion, I was following different strands of yarn back and forth through a tangled knotted ball. This went on for more than thirty minutes, but I didn't want to ask for help, so I didn't ask. However, my husband noticed my frustration and started helping me. He very patiently helped me detangle the knotted yarn so I could continue to crochet. I felt supported and cared-for in that moment. I accepted his help and decided I should learn to ask and not be so stubborn. Kangaroo Joeys are wise enough to accept help.

Kangaroo Joey, Looking Back, Your Turn

I believe my longing for attachment has been one of the driving forces in my life. This is good and healthy. As I get older, I see more and more examples of Kangaroo Joey.

Now it's your turn to write down your memories. When have you had that special bond when you felt vulnerable? When have you asked for help? Use the following space to write down your examples.

_____

_____

_____

_____

_____

_____

_____

CHAPTER 9

....

BOND KANGAROO JOEY SKILL SET, LOOKING FORWARD: KJ1, KJ2, KJ3, KJ4

One attribute of kangaroos is that they can't hop backwards, only forward. It's time for you to move forward and see which kangaroo joey skills you'd like to refine. We'll look at each of the kangaroo joey attributes from the animal skill set chart.

Kangaroo Joey 1
I Am Comfortable Asking for Help

1. *Think.* I don't have to be the hero. I don't have to be the helper. It's okay for me to ask for help.
2. *Ask. Just ask.* When you see that you need something, don't be afraid to ask. If you think it's more admirable to be the martyr, think again. Self-sacrificing can be a way to get attention and approval, but it's selfish if you use it to prove what a good person you are. Don't steal someone else's blessing by denying them the opportunity to help you.
3. *Bond.* Letting someone help you builds a bond that nothing else can. Be connected.

_____

_____

_____

_____

Take the time to write down how you feel about these ideas. It may be difficult for you to ask for help but know that it's a skill that will help you improve relationships.

_____

_____

_____

_____

Kangaroo Joey 2
I Believe that Being Vulnerable Is a Good Thing

1. *Remember.* You were born vulnerable. That's the only way you got to be stronger, by learning from parents, by learning from mistakes. It's part of the process of growing.
2. *Be honest, transparent, genuine.* Vulnerability equals integrity.
3. *Humility is good for relationships.* It levels the playing field and helps you be real and have true, trusting bonds with people.

_____
_____
_____
_____

Write down how you feel about being vulnerable.

_____
_____
_____
_____

Kangaroo Joey 3
I Value Being Connected/Attached in Relationships

1. *Think.* Together is better. Alone is lonely. Join your mind, your heart, your soul with someone else, and you are more than you were when you were alone.
2. *Remember.* Connection builds interlocking strength. "Though one may be overpowered, two can defend themselves. A cord of three strands is not quickly broken" (Ecclesiastes 4:12 NIV).
3. *It's worth the risk.* It's hard to find someone you can trust, but once you do, the bond is enriching and erases the initial fear of abandonment.

_____
_____
_____
_____

Write down your thoughts about connecting/attaching through relationships.

_____
_____
_____
_____

Bond Kangaroo Joey 4
I Find It Natural to Express Gratitude

1. *Dependent.* Admit it. We are all depending on someone or something else to keep us strong.
2. *Thank you.* Acknowledge your feeling of gratitude and tell someone you are grateful for them and what they've done to make your life better.
3. *Make a gratitude list.* Consider doing this daily. Increasing your feelings of gratitude can help you live a more positive, hopeful life.

_____
_____
_____
_____
_____

Take a few moments to start your gratitude list right now.

_____
_____
_____
_____
_____

CHAPTER 10

....

FINDING THE BOND KANGAROO JOEY BALANCE

Remember that a kangaroo joey remains inside its mother's pouch for four to fifteen months before crawling out to face life alone. There is a bond/attachment developed during this time, partly from natural proximity and partly from developmental factors. When we apply this concept to our situations, we need to figure out just how much bonding we need and how much independence we need. Bonding is the beginning but is not meant to be permanent entrapment. Having Bond Kangaroo Joey in your life is essential, but how much is beneficial? Consider the following discussion to help you figure out where you are on the bond kangaroo joey scale.

The Benefits of Bond

Bond is the most basic attachment need. It begins in the beginning, when you are a tiny baby seeking the love and care of a parent. Bonding is essential and helps to lay the foundation for future healthy relationships. When a secure attachment is formed, a baby will thrive and develop trust in caregivers, learning to love and be loved. Bond is that quality that seeks connection and wants to be held and valued and cared for. Bond allows you to be vulnerable, to ask for help, and to receive it without feeling obligated to pay it back. Bond allows you to be grateful when you don't earn anything at all. It helps you to develop a basic sense of intrinsic significance that isn't based on work or performance. Depending on others can be difficult, but it is an act of grace and trust. Allowing yourself to receive, not just give, is a way of appreciating the generosity and compassion of others.

The Handicaps of Bond

Bond can paralyze you from becoming your true self if overused. When you connect so completely with another person, you may become enmeshed. You may never discover who you really are since you are so inseparable from this other person. You may become dependent and needy. You may feel offended when this person does not anticipate your needs. You may not consider the other person's needs because you expect them to meet your needs. You don't develop your own opinions because you are an extension of the other person and may become a puppet of their opinions. You may be afraid to do things on your own because you have never developed your own skills.

Too Much Bond

The extreme bond kangaroo joey manifestation is codependency. Needing to be cared for and needing to be needed go hand in hand. You feel it is impossible to be on your own, and the other person believes you won't survive without them. This puts a strain on both of you. Resentment is inevitable. The connection becomes a burden, and you unintentionally drain the strength from the other person. Neither one of you can thrive because you are connected in an unhealthy enmeshed relationship. Picture two trees whose roots are so entangled that neither one can grow to its potential.

Too Little Bond

When a person does not attach and seek connection, this lack of bond can result in detachment and feelings of abandonment. You may feel misunderstood and awkward in social situations. You want to be loved and connected, but you don't know how to ask for what you've never experienced yourself. You don't feel comfortable asking for help or reaching out to build relationships.

A Healthy Bond Balance

Bond Kangaroo Joey's skill works best when connected to a person who has healthy boundaries. Blending strengths without losing the essence of self is imperative. Think of vinegar and oil. Both are different but make a nice blend when shaken together. When at rest, the vinegar and oil separate back out and are each a distinctive, identifiable substance. This is a healthy example of interdependence. Contrast this with Kool-Aid. Once the Kool-Aid powder is mixed with water, there is no separating it back out. This is an example of codependence, which is not healthy. Maintain your sense of self or you will be lost in the mix.

Here are some questions to help you figure out what your bond kangaroo joey factor may be.

1. Do you feel comfortable disagreeing with someone you love? Do you trust that they will still love you through the disagreement?
   If your answer is yes to both questions, give yourself five points.
   If your answer is no to one question, give yourself six points.
   If your answer is no to both questions, give yourself seven points.
   Your answer: _____
2. Do you hesitate to do things on your own? Do you worry that you may not be able to handle daily life challenges?
   If your answer is no to both questions, give yourself five points.
   If your answer is yes to one question, give yourself four points.

If your answer is yes to both questions, give yourself three points.
Your answer: _____

3. Do you push people away when they offer to help you? Do you think you can't trust anyone?
   If your answer is no to both questions, give yourself five points.
   If your answer is yes to one question, give yourself six points.
   If your answer is yes to both questions, give yourself seven points.
   Your answer: _____

4. Do you have difficulty figuring out what you like? Do you go along with what your loved one likes?
   If your answer is no to both questions, give yourself five points.
   If your answer is yes to one question, give yourself four points.
   If your answer is yes to both questions, give yourself three points.
   Your answer: _____

5. Do you find yourself making plans without considering your loved ones? Do you usually prefer to do your own separate activities?
   If your answer is no to both questions, give yourself five points.
   If your answer is yes to one question, give yourself six points.
   If your answer is yes to both questions s, give yourself seven points.
   Your answer: _____

6. Do you believe you have grown emotionally from being in a relationship? Has this bond enhanced your potential rather than stunted your growth?
   If your answer is yes to both questions, give yourself five points.
   If your answer is yes to one question, give yourself four points.
   If your answer is no to both questions, give yourself six points.
   Your answer: _____

7. Do you treasure the moments you spend attached as well as the moments you do things independently? Do you miss your person when you are apart yet accept that the separation is temporary? Do you experience joy when reunited but feel comfortable planning time for separate activities and interests?
   If your answer is yes to all these questions, give yourself five points.
   If your answer is no, I'd rather be independent and alone, give yourself six points.
   If your answer is no, I don't feel comfortable doing anything on my own, give yourself four points.
   Your answer: _____

Your overall bond kangaroo joey score

1. _____ 2._____ 3._____ 4._____ 5._____ 6._____ 7._____
_____Total divided by seven =_____

Bond Kangaroo Joey Skill: Conclusion/Summary/Recommendations

If your average score is 5, congratulations, you are a super bond kangaroo joey!

If your average score is less than 5, you may need to coax your kangaroo joey out of its pouch.

Suggestions: Go to the grocery store by yourself. Find a hobby that you do just for you. Be brave enough to state your own opinion.

Bottom line: Do anything that will help you temporarily separate from your attachment to that one special person.

If your average score is more than 5, you may need to get your kangaroo joey back in the pouch.

Suggestions: Spend some one-on-one time with someone (spouse, significant other). Make a list of the things you appreciate about this most attached person. Go on a road trip with this person.

Bottom line: Do anything that will draw you closer to the person you are closest to. You may need to rekindle the attachment and learn to be bonded to them all over again.

Nurture Elephant (Drawn by Leslie Kirkes)

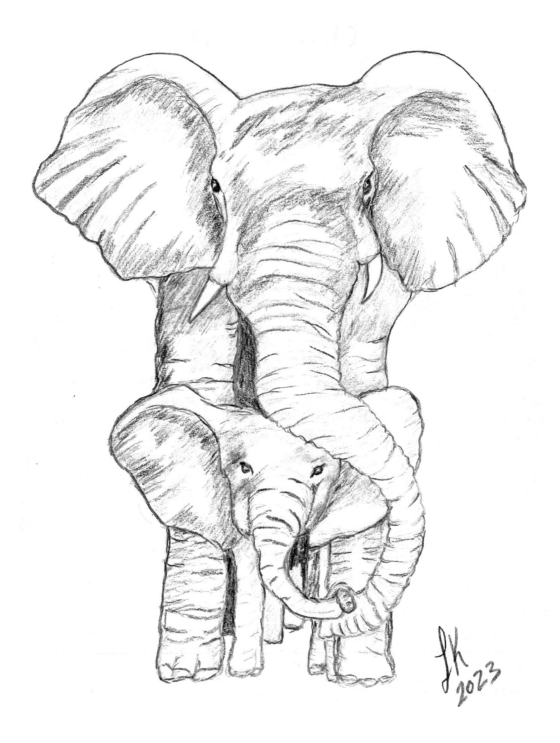

CHAPTER 11

....

NURTURE ELEPHANT, LOOKING BACK

For I desire steadfast love and not sacrifice, the knowledge of God rather than burnt offerings.
—Hosea 6:6 ESV

Nurture Elephant Skill

The nurture elephant skill represents the drive to reach out and care for others, often at the risk of self. Elephants protect and nurture; they take care of their babies and focus on others. They have the longest known gestation period (twenty-two months). Their babies are born almost blind, and the mother will often nurse the baby for up to six years. When a new elephant mother gives birth, the strongest elephants circle up to protect her and her baby. They face outwards and kick and stomp to scare predators away. When baby elephants are left as orphans, other elephants readily adopt them. Elephants are intelligent, protective, and connected to their herd as well as to their babies. Elephants even mourn their dead. Nurture Elephant is a caregiver who sometimes gets frustrated and defensive for lack of self-care. This elephant builds others up and sometimes risks danger to create a haven of safety. When you feel the impulse to nurture, picture Nurture Elephant in your mind.

Looking Back
Examples of My Nurture Elephant Moments

This is my favorite crutch, and I like to think I'm a nurturer. I scored three out of four elephant nurture qualities on the animal skill set chart. There is one drawback however. I often do for others without taking care of myself first. I have learned to "love your neighbor as yourself," but in my mind, it often translates as "love your neighbor instead of yourself." Sometimes, caring for others feels more like an obligation than an act of loving nurture. I realize this is a wonderful gift to have if I don't neglect my own needs.

Caring for my baby brother

I wanted a baby brother, so I ordered one out of the Sears catalog. That didn't work, so I ordered one out of the Montgomery Ward catalog. Finally, when I was four and a half years old, my baby brother arrived, and I became a big sister, at last. I wanted to care for my baby brother and give him all the love and attention he needed. I got him out of his crib one day and accidentally dropped him on his head! I don't remember how long he cried; I don't remember what my parents said about it. Now I realize I was a baby elephant trying to grow up too soon. I was Nurture Elephant in-training, and forgot I was the big sister, not the mother. I worried about my brother for a long time, but he has forgiven me and turned out okay.

Babysitter/Homemaker

When there were five of us kids, it became more difficult for all of us to go to a babysitter after school. Mom decided to find a responsible teenager to go to the house and watch us until she got off work each day. It didn't take long for me to realize that I knew more than the new babysitter. I told Mom that the babysitter didn't even know how to use a can opener. She didn't even know how to cook! One day, she tried to frost a cake while the cake was still hot out of the oven. That was the last straw for me! So I asked Mom if I could be the babysitter. With three brothers and one baby sister (ten years younger than I), I quickly latched onto my new role. I felt comfortable cooking and cleaning and taking care of their needs. Sometimes, I felt overwhelmed because it was difficult to control three brothers who sometimes overpowered me. However, I didn't back down from this new role. It was what I had been training for. Nurture Elephant in me was beginning to thrive.

Cooking and sewing for the family

In addition to babysitting, I learned more nurturing skills. Mom and my 4-H teacher taught me how to cook. Each day at 5:00 p.m., I had supper on the table when Mom got home from work. I enjoyed making biscuits or tortillas almost every day and planning delicious desserts to finish-off each meal. I learned to sew in 4-H, so I began to make Mom's nursing uniforms, my own clothes, and clothes for my little sister. I enjoyed nurturing my family by caring for their needs.

College caregiving

I attended Warren Wilson College in Swannanoa, North Carolina, where everyone earned their room and board by working fifteen hours per week. I expressed an interest in becoming the seamstress of the drama department. This job choice seemed perfect for me because it gave me the opportunity to design and sew costumes for all the students in the plays. I tried to tailor each garment to the needs of the person who wore it. For me, it was an act of caring for individual people, not just a sewing project.

After two years, I got to choose a second job. I became breakfast supervisor of the dining hall. I was responsible for cooking breakfast for everyone. I felt a sense of pride and responsibility as I cared for so many hungry students. As breakfast supervisor, I was responsible for supervising the other students who worked in the dining hall with me. Sometimes, I had to call them to get them up in the morning so they would come to work. This reminded me of my big sister role when I was still at home.

Another reason I chose this college was that every student was required to do a service project before graduating. I chose to involve myself in the Laubach literacy program. This was an outreach program to teach adults how to read. My nurture elephant thrived as a teacher and an encourager of adults who had never had the opportunity to go to school when they were young.

Teacher/Nurturer

After I graduated from college with a BA in elementary education, my first job was as a second grade teacher for two years in Lordsburg, New Mexico. I wanted to teach and nurture all these kids and was discouraged that I couldn't save them all. I remember one little boy who disregarded every rule and was aggressive to other children. I kept him in at recess and observed a significant transformation in his behavior. He was cooperative and sweet when he was alone with me. It was then that I realized I preferred helping kids with their family problems and psychological needs. I attended Western New Mexico University in Silver City and received my master's degree in guidance and counseling. Nurture Elephant was stepping up to take its place in a more focused way.

The ultimate nurturing experience

For fifteen years, I stayed home with my own four kids, loving, nurturing, and bonding with them. This was my most fulfilling role in my whole life. It was what I'd always wanted for myself and attempted to give to them. It was harder for me to let go of them than it was for them to let go of me. Sending them off to school was challenging, especially when my youngest child, my little boy, went to kindergarten and had to console me that it was going to be okay. One day, I was late to the bus stop and chased the bus all the way back to school. I was frantic with worry that he would be traumatized, and I had to get him back in my possession immediately. I was angry that the bus driver wouldn't stop, but he explained to me that he wasn't allowed to let any child off the bus except at their assigned bus stop or back at the school. Mama Nurture Elephant inside me was quite intimidating, but it didn't change the situation. I had made a mistake, and I couldn't undo the mistake of being late. However, I wanted to minimize the effects of the emotional trauma if possible.

Rescuing my children from a rattlesnake

This event may represent the nurture elephant skill, but it's also one of my rare lion-hearted spurts of bravery. One day, I was watering the plants we had planted outside our house. I heard a sound that I thought was a leaky garden hose. I followed the sound and was shocked to find a rattlesnake in my children's playhouse. It was rattling, and I was afraid it would bite me or my kids. My husband was at work and couldn't come home, so I knew I had to protect my kids. I sent all four kids inside. They all watched from the bedroom window as I felt compelled to destroy the danger rattling in my territory, my children's territory. It took several rocks, a shovel, and a hoe, but when I was done, the snake was fully dead. I hung it on the barbed-wire fence as a symbol of victory.

Becoming a professional nurturer

My priority after I got married was to nurture my own children. I had put my counseling career on hold until my kids were in school. When my youngest child was in first grade, I started applying for jobs as a school counselor. It seemed that the schools didn't want to hire me since I had been "out of commission" for fifteen years. So at thirty-nine years old, I started working at Bethel Baptist Counseling Ministry where I got the supervision required to be a mental health counselor rather than a school counselor. During the next ten years, I went on to work in a juvenile facility as a counselor for wayward teenage boys and then worked at a community mental health agency. At that point, I had the experience to start my own independent practice. Nurture Elephant was now full-grown. For eighteen more years, I had a busy counseling business of my own. I felt very comfortable in the nurturing role of counselor. Caring for my clients suited me very well since I had the need to listen, guide, protect, and nurture. It was the perfect job for me since I could see the transition and growth of my clients and could then send them out into the world stronger and more self-reliant.

Grandmother elephant

My grandchildren are quickly filling that nurture elephant role in me once again. We have a house in New Mexico and a house in Oklahoma. I sometimes go through "grandmother withdrawals" when we are in Oklahoma. When I'm in New Mexico, I love to go visit my children and grandchildren so I can care, connect, and encourage them.

Nurture, side by side

I also find that my husband still needs me to help him with medical issues and companionship. We are growing closer through the years, and it seems we need each other even more as we grow older. Nurturing side by side helps my elephant heart to sing.

Nurture Elephant, Looking Back, Your Turn

Now it's time for you to think of your nurturing moments. Please write them down in the space that follows.

_____

_____

_____

CHAPTER 12

....

NURTURE ELEPHANT SKILL SET, LOOKING FORWARD: E1, E2, E3, E4

From my examples, and probably from your own, as well, it is easy to see how nurturing can be a great skill but can also stifle the growth of the ones we are trying to nurture if we over-protect and over-nurture. Let's look at each of the positive characteristics of the Nurture Elephant from the Animal Skill Set Chart. Even if you are not a natural Nurture Elephant, you can find these skills to be beneficial.

Elephant 1
My First Impulse Is to Care for Others

1. *Remember.* There are others who may not be as strong or experienced as you are. Reach out to help them.
2. *Relationships hinge on mutual caring.* Follow the Golden Rule: Do for others as you would have them do for you.
3. *Don't overthink it.* Just do what needs to be done to fill the gap to care for those in need.

_____

_____

_____

_____

_____

Now write down your thoughts. Does caring for others come naturally to you?

_____

_____

_____

_____

_____

Elephant 2
I Am Good at Teaching and Nurturing

1. *Think*: Even if you don't think you're good at teaching, you are a teacher and an example to people around you. Practice teaching and nurturing a child to discover you may have this ability.
2. *If you already think you're good at teaching, take a step back to listen.* Listen to your students and try to understand what they really need, not just what you want to teach.
3. *Nurturing is more than teaching.* It doesn't have a set agenda. Nurturing has the best interests of the other person in mind, always.

_____

_____

_____

_____

_____

Now write down your thoughts about your role as a teacher and nurturer below.

_____

_____

_____

_____

Elephant 3
I Am Generous with My Time, Ideas, and Possessions

1. *Time.* Time is precious. It is a gift we receive every day, twenty-four hours a day. Are you willing to donate part of your time to address the needs of someone else? Consider it.
2. *Ideas.* Ideas come and go. Some are brilliant; some are mundane. Are you willing to share these ideas with others? They may help to enlighten or encourage someone.
3. *Possessions.* We own things. We have money. Are you willing to share with someone less fortunate? Practice being altruistic, and you will find it's a blessing to you as well.

_____

_____

_____

_____

How are you feeling about giving to others? Write down your thoughts below.

_____
_____
_____
_____
_____

Elephant 4
I Am a Natural Advocate for Other People

1. *Stand up for others.* Help them to find their own strength but speak up for them until they can advocate for themselves.
2. *Look around you.* Find an injustice that has been overlooked. Find someone who has been ignored. See if you can help that person, one-on-one.
3. *Broaden your perspective.* Don't think only about your own needs. Put yourself in someone else's shoes for a moment.

_____
_____
_____
_____

Write down how you feel about being an advocate for someone.

_____
_____
_____
_____

CHAPTER 13

....

FINDING THE NURTURE ELEPHANT BALANCE

At first glance, Nurture Elephant seems to be totally virtuous. This is true when the motives are pure, and Nurture Elephant has healthy boundaries. On the other hand, if Nurture Elephant oversteps its limits, it can become a detriment. Think about the following ideas to see if you may have too much or too little of Nurture Elephant in your life.

The Benefits of Nurture

Nurture Elephant builds others up and always put others first. You always have someone to care for, and you have a tender, compassionate heart. You notice the needs of others and are always planning ways to help them out. You may feel responsible for guiding and nurturing others, protecting, and shielding them from harm. Usually, you take charge of situations when you notice there is a need for emotional or physical support. You may provide for someone who is young, sick, unfortunate, going through a disaster, or needing support in other ways. You are an encourager and champion of lost causes. You rescue and heal and comfort others.

The Handicaps of Nurture

So much giving can burn you out. Self-sacrificing can sound like a good thing, but it can drain your energy and make you weak and cranky. You may become resentful when your help isn't appreciated. You may become overprotective and controlling, pushing your own agenda on someone who may not want what you are offering. You may enable people to depend on you instead of taking responsibility for themselves. You may neglect self-care and then blame others for not noticing what you need.

Too Much Nurture

The extreme nurture elephant is the person who refuses to let others help. Giving is the sole defining feature of this nurture elephant. Other people may avoid the elephant who always wants to change them or fix them or control them. Relationships are always upside down because Nurture Elephant must be in front and can never receive advice or help from anyone else. Nurture Elephant is the authority on everyone else's needs and can't fathom being wrong or needing anything from anyone else. This overly zealous elephant needs to be needed and doesn't know how to be nurtured in return.

Too Little Nurture

Without the nurture skill, you can become selfish and lonely. You will never volunteer to help anyone but will always think it's someone else's job. You may expect others to take care of you, but you would never think of returning the favor. You may think nurturing is a nuisance and have little patience for people who are needy or going through difficult times.

A Healthy Nurture Balance

The best use of the nurture elephant skill is to reach out with a helping hand but to respect the preferences of the ones you are helping. Allowing them to be part of the healing process, instead of taking over as an authority figure, will be most beneficial. You will learn to step back and watch people take steps on their own instead of leading them by the hand when your help is no longer necessary. You will learn to accept help from others and take the time to care for yourself as well.

Consider the following questions as you assess your "nurture factor."

1. Do you genuinely care for others? Do you help them when you see they have a need?
   If your answer is yes to both questions, give yourself five points.
   If your answer is no to one question, give yourself six points.
   If your answer is no to both questions, give yourself seven points.
   Your answer: _____
2. Do you expect people to show their appreciation? Do you want a thank you every time you help someone?
   If your answer is no to both questions, give yourself five points.
   If your answer is yes to one question, give yourself four points,
   If your answer is yes to both questions, give yourself three points.
   Your answer: _____
3. Do you ignore requests for help? Do you think people should always help themselves?
   If your answer is no to both questions, give yourself five points.
   If your answer is yes to one question, give yourself six points.
   If your answer is yes to both questions, give yourself seven points.
   Your answer: _____
4. Do you feel compelled to say "yes" every time someone asks for help? Do you push yourself to help even when you feel the burden of too much helping?
   If your answer is no to both questions, give yourself five points.

If your answer is yes to one question, give yourself four points.

If your answer is yes to both questions, give yourself three points.

Your answer: _____

5. Do you usually say "no" when asked to volunteer for community benevolence projects? Do you think it's more important to mind your own business?

If your answer is no to both questions, give yourself five points.

If your answer is yes to one question, give yourself six points.

If you're answer is yes to both questions, give yourself seven points.

Your answer: _____

6. Do you ask how you can help? Do you trust the person to know what they need?

If your answer is yes to both questions, give yourself five points.

If your answer is no to one question, give yourself four points.

If your answer is no to both questions, give yourself three points.

Your answer: _____

7. Do you love helping others but know where to set limits? Do you realize that too much help can be enabling? Do you take the time to care for yourself and your family?

If you can answer yes to all three questions, give yourself five points.

If you would like to help, but prioritize your own family's needs instead, give yourself six points.

If you feel so compelled to help that you neglect yourself and your family, give yourself four points.

Your answer: _____

Your overall nurture elephant score

Tally up your answers from all seven questions. Then average them by dividing your total score by seven.

1._____ 2._____ 3._____ 4._____ 5._____ 6._____ 7._____
_____Total divided by seven =_____

Nurture Elephant: Conclusion/Summary/Recommendations

If your average score is 5, congratulations, you are a super nurture elephant!

If your average score is less than 5, your nurture elephant is overworking.

Suggestions: Let your "yes be yes and your no be no." Your "yes" needs to be wholehearted. Force yourself to do a self-care activity. Spend time with your family instead of going out to help someone.

Bottom line: Do anything that will dial-down your compulsion for nurturing others.

If your average score is more than 5, your nurture elephant needs to be stimulated.

Suggestions: Say "yes" when you are asked to volunteer your time to help needy people. Find someone to mentor, teaching them a skill you possess. Spend time with someone who needs encouragement.

Bottom line: Do any activity that stretches your empathy, that challenges you to think about others instead of yourself.

Escape Cat (Drawn by Elia Weeks)

CHAPTER 14

....

ESCAPE CAT, LOOKING BACK

*No temptation has overtaken you that is not common to man. God is faithful,
and He will not let you be tempted beyond your ability, but with the temptation
He will also provide a way of escape, that you may be able to endure it.*
—1 Corinthians 10:13 ESV

Escape Cat Skill

The escape cat skill represents the inclination to run away or escape. Cats will avoid problems at all costs to secure a place of perceived safety. Their impulse is to escape danger or pain by leaving the scene of the trauma. Cats are escape artists who quickly climb to the tops of trees where pursuers can't follow. From that vantage point, they can patiently watch and reflect as they contemplate the next move. Cats are detached, independent, creative, and self-reliant. They seek an environment of comfort and self-satisfaction. This ability to separate from the race, to relax and "take a catnap" can be a very good thing. Perhaps this is why cats have the reputation of having "nine lives," evading danger and cheating death multiple times. Resilience and dexterity are wonderful attributes of Escape Cat. However, when escape skills are taken too far, an Escape Cat could get stuck in a tree, or stuck in a make-believe place where fantasy and denial rule. When you feel the impulse to escape, picture Escape Cat in your mind.

Looking Back
Examples of My Escape Cat Moments

I scored two out of four Escape Cat qualities on the animal skill set chart. I was surprised to find how many of these Escape Cat maneuvers I have utilized throughout my life. Some of them have been helpful diversions. Others have been attempts to deflect and deny real issues that needed to be dealt with. Join me as I reflect and remember.

Missing the school bus on purpose

Starting school was scary for me. There wasn't such a thing as kindergarten in Reserve, New Mexico in 1961, so first grade was my first school experience. To make it even worse, my first-grade teacher was mean. She tied kids to their desks and said she had eyes in the back of her head. My biggest fear was that I would be the next kid she decided to punish. I was terrified and finally thought of a plan. The only solution I knew would work was not to be in that classroom. One morning, I obediently walked to the bus stop about a quarter mile from the house. I was confident that my parents didn't know about my plan. Then I hid behind the gate as soon as I saw the bus coming. I breathed a big sigh of relief and started to relax as the bus drove out of sight. At that moment, I realized the problem with my plan. I hadn't figured out what to do next. Sure enough, Mom saw me when she was driving by the bus stop on her way to work. She insisted that she would take me to school late. She assured me that I could avoid punishment by maintaining my pattern of good behavior. I wasn't sure about that, but I had no choice. I didn't get to stay home alone. I didn't get to escape the reality of school and that dreaded first grade teacher. My mother was right. I didn't get tied to my desk. That didn't stop me from worrying all the rest of that school year however. At the end of the school year, the teacher got fired. That was not much consolation to me, but thankfully, I had the best teacher ever when I got to second grade.

Colorful escape artist

Coloring was one of my favorite distractions, probably because my mother would sit and color with me. I didn't like the constraints of staying within the lines of the picture, but I overcame that barrier by blending colors within the picture. In more recent years, I've realized the importance of having a frame for your picture, a limit on the outside, so that you can be ultimately creative on the inside. I've never thought of myself as an artist, but I love creative doodling and watercolor mirages. I didn't know it as a child, but I was developing the creative, emotional side of my brain by coloring. It was an escape from all the logical, cognitive thoughts that seemed so burdensome.

Vicarious reading

I was shy and somewhat of a dreamer. I went to school, did my chores, and read books. The bookmobile was my supplier. I lived my life through the books I was reading. I felt closer to the characters in the books than I did to people in my real life. I could imagine the victories and the failures and live my life vicariously through their stories. I even learned to mispronounce some words through my self-taught process. I knew exactly what the words meant, but I had my own special way of pronouncing them. Two examples were pronouncing jeopardy as "GEE-oh-party" and algebra as "Al-JEB-ra" with the accent on the middle syllable. I didn't realize I was mispronouncing the words because I didn't use the words in conversations with real people. I was content carrying on imaginary conversations with imaginary people who mispronounced words the same way I did. Books allowed me to escape the challenge of real-life interactions and helped fill my time with fantasy and imagination.

Excuse me, I'm invisible

People were somewhat scary to me. I heard kids at school whispering that I was stuck-up, but I was really just scared they would reject me. I used to swing as high as I could on the swings in the school playground. My mom's public health office was visible from that vantage point, so I imagined that she would come and rescue me from the peers that felt so distant.

Body image delusions

As a child, I was told that I was "pleasingly plump," but I was not pleased. When I was in sixth grade, I overheard a boy say that he would like me "if I was not so fat." That's when I began to believe the delusion that if I was tall and skinny, I would be accepted. I fabricated ways to trick myself into believing I was okay with myself. I would shop for clothes that had a smaller size tag so I could pretend I had lost weight. I prided myself on having small feet, but then I hurt my feet by cramming my toes into shoes that were too small. I tried to lose weight by going on daily runs and by going on strict, unreasonable diets. One diet was to eat nothing but boiled eggs and oranges. To get enough calcium, the diet recommended that you eat one crunched-up eggshell each day. Perhaps that's why I don't like eggs to this day. Another diet recommended that you weigh everything you eat and figure out the calories before you put anything in your mouth. None of these diets helped me lose weight. I was feeling more and more discouraged.

Finally, a doctor tested my thyroid and found out that I suffer from hypothyroidism. Then I got on thyroid medication and found it easier to manage my weight. I still felt "fat" and had a love/hate relationship with food for many years. Now I realize that all types of eating disorders are an escape from self-acceptance. They set unrealistic standards that can never be met. It's the ultimate self-sabotage. For me, it gave me an excuse to avoid relationships even further. I found myself unacceptable, so I reasoned falsely that others would come to the same conclusion. The miracle was that growing up, getting married and having my own children taught me how wrong I was when I was stuck in this delusion.

False significance through academic achievement

I needed to feel significant in some way, so I poured myself into my studies. I ignored the social scene and climbed the academic ladder. I was often known as "teacher's pet" and decided that was good enough. My mother's family is from a long line of valedictorians and salutatorians. I wanted to follow in my mother's footsteps, so I set my goal to be valedictorian of my class. I did achieve that goal but minimized it in my mind somewhat since my senior class consisted of only nineteen students.

Achieving this honor did help me escape to the greater world of college. I was like Escape Cat scrambling up a tree to get a new perspective. I felt a sense of safety in a new place, three thousand miles away from home. From the vantage point of college, I could see myself as the person I'd always wanted to be. I had escaped from the familiarity of a past world that knew me for the imperfect person I had always thought I was.

Acting the part

Now that I was in college, I used a familiar escape skill that helped me in high school, wearing emotional masks, pretending I was confident. I did a flashback to my junior year of high school and remembered my first acting role as "Little Allergy" in the play *Beware the Bear*. It was then that I read the script and stepped into the story, just like I did when I read books, with one difference. I could speak out loud and let my imagination go one step further. I went on to be in several plays in college. My favorite role was as Cecily Cardew in the Oscar Wilde play *The Importance of Being Earnest*. I discovered that I could be brave or sociable or whatever the script asked of me. Pretending to be the person in the play helped me to discover the attributes I had but didn't normally access. It gave me the opportunity to "try on" different attitudes and mannerisms and practice being the self I wanted to be in real life. The whole process was serendipity at its finest.

Musical counterpoint

Music has been a fantasy world for me—a way of escaping into a world of self-expression that feels safer than talking. Singing gives me a voice that can fly above the fears of normal interactive communication. Playing my flute in high school gave me access to a place of acceptance, as a member of a team—a band marching to the same drummer. Playing the piano is purely therapeutic for me. I enjoy playing simple songs and singing along. Music is the language of my soul—the words that escape normal conversation.

Dancing diversion

When I met my husband, we would go dancing almost every weekend. It was a way of connecting that made me forget about myself. I loved the rhythm, the lyrics, and the fact that I could forget everything else. Any differences we had seemed to disappear. The synchronized steps and harmony of the music erased any thoughts of discord.

Puzzles/Board games

Puzzles and board games have always been fun activities for me. We didn't have television until I was in high school, so playing board games was my favorite family time. Work was the priority, so playing games was an unnecessary pleasure that seemed like an escape, a reward, or bonus. I was never very competitive, so I never really cared whether I won or lost. That's probably why I like puzzles so much because it's a team effort without so many rules to follow. To this day, my parents always have a puzzle in progress when we go visit, and I have extended the family tradition.

Burying my head in the sand

While I was actively engaged as a counselor, I successfully managed not to read reviews of my business. My fear of rejection (and one negative review many years ago) has contributed to my justification of not reading reviews at all. I say that "I'm old-school, and I don't need reviews." I say, "People rig the reviews, and you can't trust them." I say, "My business is thriving, so what's the point of reading reviews?" So what's the point? The point I must make when I take a transparent look at myself is that I am a coward and like to be in denial sometimes. The fear of rejection can be sidestepped if you pretend that you don't care what people think. The truth is that I care too much about what people think. Seeking approval has been one of the driving forces in my life. Now that I'm no longer in business, I realize that my fear was unrealistic. Sometimes Escape Cat avoids perceived confrontation and never knows what real opportunities might be around the corner.

Did the cat get my tongue?

Now that I am retired, my husband and I have two homes in two different states. Our Oklahoma home is perfect for my husband's health, and our New Mexico home keeps us connected to family. Lots of new neighbors, right? Yes, but not exactly. I do know I have neighbors living in the houses all up and down the streets. Have I knocked on any doors? Have I reached out to make friends? No. I do respond when people reach out to me, but I do not try to reach out to them. Again, I have my excuses. I tell myself that I don't need friends, and I don't have time for them. I tell myself that my husband and family are all I need. I tell myself that I don't want to connect with them because I will just leave to go to the other house and then offend a potential friend. What's the truth? I would rather be comfortable in my safe, little, sometimes lonely shell than take a chance on being rejected (or accepted). I am acutely aware that I am outside my comfort zone. I was very comfortable talking to people for one hour a week, week after week. I was very comfortable sharing my thoughts, my emotions, my stories, and my life when I was in that comfortable chair in that comfortable office. So now I need to find a comfortable place inside myself—a place where I can be the self I was when I was in that counselor chair. I need to leave Escape Cat at home and go out to explore "a beautiful day in the neighborhood."

Escape Cat, Looking Back, Your Turn

I am amazed to see such a myriad of diversions and self-care options I had forgotten about. However, I see a common theme: I find solace in avoiding people. That is an insight that I have been avoiding most of my life. When I get to know people, I feel comfortable sharing and helping and connecting with them. That's why I loved having clients to talk to on a regular, scheduled basis. Now that I don't have that "crutch," I need to develop more intentional connections with people so that I won't be that cat stuck in a tree watching the people go by. What about you? Do you see any patterns of escape in your life? Please use the space below to record your own thoughts and memories.

_____

_____

_____

_____

_____

_____

_____

_____

_____

_____

_____

_____

_____

_____

_____

_____

_____

_____

_____

_____

_____

_____

_____

_____

_____

_____

_____

_____

_____

_____

_____

_____

_____

_____

_____

_____

_____

_____

_____

_____

CHAPTER 15

ESCAPE CAT SKILL SET, LOOKING FORWARD: C1, C2, C3, C4

Escaping is sometimes good and sometimes not so good. Either way, looking forward is the next best thing to do. Evaluate yourself according to the escape cat skills from the animal skill set chart. You can benefit from these skills even if Escape Cat is not your natural first response.

Cat 1
I Know When I Need to Escape/Get Away

1. *Remember.* Sometimes, it is best to leave the scene. Sometimes, you must admit there is nothing you can do if you stick around. It is not weak; it is wise. You can take the time to strengthen yourself and evaluate options while you gain a more objective perspective from a distance.
2. *Think.* I don't have to be the hero. Sometimes, behind-the-scenes thinking is better.
3. *Recoup.* You will benefit from taking a break and renewing your strength. You can do an even better job when you return to your normal routine.

_____
_____
_____
_____
_____

Write down how you are feeling about the idea of escape as a positive thing.

_____
_____
_____
_____

Cat 2
I Am Good at Self-Soothing and Self-Care

1. *Think.* Taking care of yourself is not selfish. It is proactive and healthy. You can't take care of anyone else if you don't take care of yourself first.
2. *Relax.* Picture all the most calming things you can imagine. Let your imagination take you to that soothing place for at least fifteen minutes. Gently detach yourself from your worries and concerns.
3. *Practice self-care.* Evaluate yourself to see if you are taking care of your mind, body, emotions, and spirit. Learn to establish a daily ritual of self-care activities.

_____

_____

_____

_____

_____

List the things you are already doing to soothe and care for yourself. Think of some additional ways you could care for yourself even more effectively.

_____

_____

_____

_____

Cat 3
I Am Creative and Have Hobbies

1. *Remember.* Everyone has different natural abilities. You just need to find some skills and activities that give you joy and purpose. It may even be something work-related if you take the time to relax and enjoy the process.
2. *Don't put creativity in a box.* Use your imagination to find the ways your brain likes to create. Every human brain has a right side and a left side. The right side of your brain is the side that is more emotional and creative whereas the left side is more logical and linear. Explore the right side of your brain to find the creative release that inspires you. It may be gardening, building, cooking, drawing, sewing, crocheting, writing, or anything you can think of.
3. *Hobbies.* Go one step further. Not only do you need to think of creative things to do but find ways to do these creative things on a regular basis. It could be a sports activity or crafting or a book club or collecting old coins. It just needs to be something you enjoy that takes your brain away from the ordinary stressors of daily life.

_____

_____

_____
_____
_____

What thoughts come to mind? Are you groping for half-fulfilled ideas that haven't surfaced? Are you feeling too busy to escape from the daily work routine? List some ideas below.

_____
_____
_____
_____

Cat 4
I Am a Visionary Who Can See the Best in a Situation

1. *Think positive.* See the silver lining in every cloud. What do you have to lose? If you have positive expectations, you won't waste your energy worrying over the worst-case scenario.
2. *Believe.* There is always hope no matter how bad a situation can get. Don't limit yourself to your own human resources. Know that God has better plans and has the power to fulfill them.
3. *Look under the surface.* Things are not always the way they appear to be. There is good that is buried, hidden, tarnished. It is your job to dig it out and shine it up.

_____
_____
_____
_____

Does it come naturally for you to think this way? Write down how you think you could apply this positive thinking to your life.

_____
_____
_____
_____
_____
_____
_____
_____

CHAPTER 16

....

FINDING THE ESCAPE CAT BALANCE

Whether you are an escape cat to the core or just adopting some of the escape skills, you may find it helpful to find your escape cat balance.

The Benefits of Escape

There is a time when fleeing is the best option. Getting away from danger and then regrouping may be the reason cats are said to have "nine lives." Making a quick getaway can ensure more time to take care of yourself and define your own goals. It is a way of distracting yourself from things that get in the way of your own needs. Escape gives you an internal focus on independent, personal priorities, realizing you can't save everyone, so you've got to save yourself. This can take the form of creative pursuits that take you away from troubling thoughts. It can keep you in a safe cocoon of self-indulgent fantasy or visual imagery that has a calming effect on your brain and your body. Relaxation and frequent catnaps can renew a tired spirit and rekindle the joy of fun and curiosity.

The Handicaps of Escape

Running away sometimes turns into deceptive and irresponsible behaviors. Self-preservation can turn into self-absorption. Fantasy gone too far can be a form of denial and avoidance of reality. Thinking only of yourself can make you seem detached and disinterested in others. Seeking pleasure and avoidance of pain can become addictive.

Too Much Escape

Becoming the quintessential escape cat could be a detriment. You may be unmotivated, self-absorbed, entitled, and distracted from the realities of life. You may be a brilliant artist or dreamer who loses touch with relationships and practical pursuits. You may prefer independent activities that are relaxing and pleasurable to group efforts that are demanding and interactive. Your natural curiosity and microscopic attention to detail may lend itself to research and design but not to the application of these discoveries. You will seek pleasure and avoid pain, choosing to live in an imaginary fairy-tale world where escape is the primary means of survival.

Too Little Escape

Without some escape cat skills in your life, you will probably be a workaholic. You will never find the end of a workday, never look forward to vacations, and find it hard to relax. You will push away pleasure and keep marching forward, never stopping to smell the roses along the way. You may lose a sense of wonder and creativity, focusing only on measurable objectives that are predictable and standard procedure. You may forget how to smile because of your serious demeanor.

A Healthy Escape Balance

Everyone needs some stress relief, and that's what Escape Cat can do for you. Working too hard for too long without a break can be very detrimental to your health and your attitude. When you schedule some "down time" into your life, it is like the ebb and flow of the ocean. It is calming, renewing, detoxifying and improves work productivity.

Here are some questions that should help you figure out what your "escape factor" may be.

1. Do you feel a sense of resiliency in your life? Do you accept difficulty with an attitude of grace and patience?

    If your answer is yes to both questions, give yourself five points.

    If your answer is no to one question, give yourself six points.

    If your answer is no to both questions, give yourself seven points.

    Your answer: _____

2. Do you find yourself making up excuses to skip work? Do you think relaxing is more important than work?

    If your answer is no to both questions, give yourself five points.

    If your answer is yes to one question, give yourself four points.

    If your answer is yes to both questions, give yourself three points.

    Your answer: _____

3. Do you find it difficult to leave work on time? Do you often work on weekends to meet deadlines?

    If your answer is no to both questions, give yourself five points.

    If your answer is yes to one question, give yourself six points.

    If your answer is yes to both questions, give yourself seven points.

    Your answer: _____

4. Do you have habits that distract you from your work? Do you often forget obligations and/ or responsibilities?

    If your answer is no to both questions, give yourself five points.

    If your answer is yes to one question, give yourself four points.

If your answer is yes to both questions, give yourself three points.

Your answer: _____

5. Do you feel overworked and frustrated? Do you feel guilty taking a break?

If your answer is no to both questions, give yourself five points.

If your answer is yes to one question, give yourself six points.

If your answer is yes to both questions, give yourself seven points.

Your answer: _____

6. Do you enjoy purposeful work? Do you look forward to hobbies and fun activities?

If your answer is yes to both questions, give yourself five points.

If your answer is yes to question one, but no to question two, give yourself six points.

If your answer is yes to question two, but no to question one, give yourself four points.

Your answer: _____

7. Do you find joy in small things? Do you notice beautiful things in your environment? Do you take the time to do self-care without feeling guilty? Do you laugh at your mistakes and keep trying without obsessing? Do you pace yourself so that you don't get exhausted when working at a difficult task?

If you can wholeheartedly answer yes to all these questions, give yourself five points.

If you think you do all these things to excess and ignore responsibilities, give yourself four points.

If you can say yes to at least three of these questions, give yourself six points.

If you answer yes to at least one question, give yourself seven points.

If you answer no to every question, give yourself eight points.

Your answer: _____

Your overall escape cat score

Tally up your answers from all seven questions. Then average them by dividing your total score by seven.

1._____ 2._____ 3._____ 4._____ 5._____ 6._____ 7._____

_____Total divided by seven =_____

Escape Cat: Conclusion/Summary/Recommendations

If your average score is 5, congratulations, you are a super escape cat!

If your average score is less than 5, you may need to block some of your cat's escape routes.

Suggestions: Set a limit on diversionary activities. Resolve to complete responsibilities before relaxing. Give up some of your self-care to attend to others.

Bottom line: Choose any activity that will help you get out of your self-centered cocoon.

If your average score is more than 5, you need to initiate more relaxation and leisure in your life.

Suggestions: Set a limit on work; stop at a scheduled time. Resolve to establish a time to relax and have fun every day. Stop worrying so much about others and do some self-care activities.

Bottom line: Choose any activity that will break the tension in your life, that will allow you to relax and unwind from the daily pressures that have imprisoned you.

Fight Lion (Drawn by Elia Weeks)

CHAPTER 17

....

FIGHT LION, LOOKING BACK

The wicked flee when no one pursues, but the righteous are bold as a lion.

—Proverbs 28:1 ESV

Fight Lion Skill

The fight lion skill represents the drive to protect and defend self or others in a crisis. It is the impulse to step up and take action, to fight the foe without retreat. Lions are brave and sometimes intimidating. Their collective roars can be heard for up to five miles as they mark their territory and define their boundaries. They are strong emergency responders that rise up and fight. They stand regally ready for defense and protection. Fight Lion represents determination, power, and courage. This lion takes charge of crises, is always assertive, and makes decisions that are strong and unvacillating. This may present as anger and an unwillingness to compromise. This lion can also be unapproachable and controlling. When you feel the impulse to fight, picture Fight Lion in your mind.

Looking Back
Examples of My Fight Lion Moments

The animal skill set chart shows that I have no fight lion qualities. I choose to believe that there is a lion inside me but one that lies sleeping most of the time. I realize that my lion needs to lift her head to see the opportunities for self-affirmation and strength and assertive choices. This is a skill I want to use more often but not in an intimidating or defensive way. Here are some examples of Fight Lion in my life as I look back.

College catapult

As I mentioned previously, excelling academically was an escape from social interaction. It was also a strong choice to work hard and move forward to effect change without having to depend on someone else. I learned that I had some academic strengths and affinities that I would never have known had I merely been escaping reality or yielding to the fear of rejection. I went from valedictorian of a class of nineteen to a college in another state, three thousand miles away. I picked out the college from a college catalog on my guidance counselor's desk. He had never heard of the college and argued that out-of-state tuition would be too expensive. I would not be dissuaded. I researched financial options and realized I could apply for a scholarship that would pay for the first year's tuition. I received that scholarship by writing an essay to convince the board that I would benefit from this college. I also received a National Honor Society scholarship. Perseverance, determination, and God's providence helped me to see that the lion in me was an overcomer that defied natural limitations. I was on my way!

Lion to lion

When my husband and I got married, we soon realized we were a case of "opposites attract." It is no secret that he is a natural lion through and through. It seemed natural to follow him and trust him. My follow dog and kangaroo joey skills seemed to complement his lion skills very well. However, I somehow knew that the dormant lion growing inside me was on the verge of exploding.

One day, about twelve years into our marriage, it did. I'll spare you the details, but we had a real confrontation, lion to lion, with my kids watching. It was terrible and humiliating and sad. I couldn't believe I had let my lion out in an aggressive way. I realized that I had been repressing resentment for far too long. As terrible as this memory is for me, it made me change. I knew I had to be more assertive every day. Being passive for so long was unhealthy. The boomerang from passive to aggressive and back was not an option. To love my husband completely, I had to learn to be honest even when I disagreed with him. This was the healthy lion option that transformed me and our marriage.

Lion confronts cow

When we lived in Tularosa, New Mexico, we had cows on our farm. One day, I noticed with alarm that our oldest daughter had gotten between a cow and her newborn baby calf. The cow was in attack mode and ran toward my daughter, trying to butt her. I ran toward the cow, screaming and waving my arms to distract her from mauling my precious daughter. Thankfully, the cow stopped in her tracks and backed away from me. My daughter was safe! She got up off the ground and ran to me. We were both shaking and crying as we hugged.

Thirty-nine and thriving

I've already told you part of my story, but here it is again from a lion's perspective. For fifteen years, I was a stay-at-home mom and felt comfortable in that cocoon. When my children went to school, my cocoon was shattered, and I had to find out if I was a butterfly strong enough to fight my way out. My first idea was to get a job as a school counselor since that is what I had trained for. Several interviews later, I got the feeling that I wasn't wanted since my degree had lain dormant for fifteen years. I briefly considered going back to teaching but knew that teaching was no longer my passion. It was then that God intervened. The director of a Christian counseling agency at our church asked if I would like to work with her. The transformation was challenging, but I managed to take those brave steps and began working at Bethel Baptist Counseling Ministry. After I got the supervision I needed, I moved on to a job as a counselor at a community residential facility for delinquent teenagers. After I took an exam to become a licensed professional clinical mental health counselor, I became the clinical director of that facility. I wanted more variety in my counseling experience, so I took a job as a counselor at a community mental health facility. It was there that I worked with more serious diagnoses and gained extensive knowledge about psychotropic medications. All along, my wings were growing, and I was becoming stronger as an individual therapist.

Braving the private practice precipice

With ten years of counseling experience behind me, I was developing a new cocoon of comfort. However, the independent, free-thinking lion inside me was beginning to have ideas of her own. Eventually, I realized there were policies and restrictions at my job that I was no longer willing to accept. I began to consider starting my own private practice. I was so scared! I was afraid that I would have no clients, that I wouldn't be able to make money, that I wouldn't be able to manage my own business. It took a lot of courage (and a lot of encouragement from my husband), but I took those brave steps. For eighteen more years, I enjoyed a busy, thriving practice that edified me and gave me a strong purpose.

Designing lion stepping out

As an individual therapist in private practice, I had many opportunities to create my own therapeutic ideas. As I look back, I realize this was the lion's influence in me. One example is when I was asked to do a training module for the Mescalero Apache Tribe. They had been having some personality conflicts in their natural resources department. I thought about using the Keirsey Temperament Sorter or another traditional personality assessment tool. I was brave enough to challenge that thought knowing I needed to tailor the training to the audience I would be serving. That's when I got the inspiration to modify the Keirsey Temperament Sorter to make it easier to implement in a work environment. I created new labels for the four basic temperament groups. Instead of the sensing/perceiving label, I created a hammer—an action figure who reacts quickly, takes control of situations, and doesn't waste time planning things out. The sensing/judging label became a measuring tape—a person who pays attention to detail and takes the time to plan and organize how ideas will be implemented. The intuitive/thinking label became a microscope, looking deeply into the inner workings of situations, analyzing and assessing them from a cognitive yet outside-the-box perspective. The intuitive/feeling label became the paint brush—a person who senses the emotions and deeper motivations of relationships, gently coaxing beauty from discord. The response from the Mescalero staff was very favorable. They identified their individual temperament groups and used this knowledge to strengthen team efforts through understanding core differences. The fight lion skill gave me the courage to blaze a new trail rather than following a beaten path.

The courage to let go

In 2008, we moved into the home I planned to live in for the rest of my life. We had a farm, site-built home, orchard, garden, and permanent security. After my husband's heart attack in 2020, we had to move to a lower elevation. Tularosa, New Mexico, at 4,500 feet elevation, was no longer the permanent retirement destination I had imagined. Pulling up roots and moving took an enormous act of courage. I have asked myself if I was merely following along (the follow dog skill) or embracing this decision and facing it with fight and fortitude. I believe that God granted me the courage to trust Him that He would go with us and protect us. His strong anchor allowed us to leave the promised land for a new land He promised. As my husband now says, "Oklahoma is God's country." At 1,200 feet elevation, he breathes better and has the energy to do all the things he can't do comfortably in New Mexico. As a concession to me, we also bought a home in Carlsbad, New Mexico, where the elevation is 3,200 feet elevation, the lowest elevation in New Mexico. We have a daughter who lives in Carlsbad, and it gives us the opportunity to visit all our family in New Mexico from that home base.

Decision to retire

This was my most difficult decision. I had to face my fear that I would lose my sense of self, that I would feel powerless and purposeless. I could see that there was a battle going on inside me that had to be resolved. Going two different directions wasn't working well despite my option to do counseling via telehealth. So I decided to take that step. It was the right time to retire. It was a lion-sized step for me, and it took me away from the chaos I was creating for myself.

Writing this book

I've always said I would like to write a book, but I never thought I would do it. Now, I am taking on that challenge. I tend to finish what I started, so this is a brave venture with enough momentum to keep rolling.

Fight Lion, Looking Back, Your Turn

It's time for you to think of your own fight lion moments. Please write them down in the following space.

_____

_____

_____

_____

_____

_____

_____

CHAPTER 18

....

FIGHT LION SKILL SET, LOOKING FORWARD: L1, L2, L3, L4

Lions charge forward in all their power and strength. Look at each of the fight lion skills on the animal skill set chart. See which ones you already have and the ones you would like to cultivate.

Lion 1
I React Quickly in a Crisis

1. *Don't stop*. React. Think on your feet. Let your first impulse be your guide.
2. *Think*: There is no time to plan or contemplate options. Let adrenaline propel you forward.
3. *Remember*. Time is critical. You must take action now. You don't have a minute to lose.

_____

_____

_____

_____

_____

Quickly brainstorm your thoughts and feelings about these guidelines. Think about how this skill could help you even if it is not your normal way of responding.

_____

_____

_____

_____

Lion 2
I Am Brave and Know When to Take Risks

1. *Remember*: Being brave means facing your fears, doing the most difficult things. Yes, you may be afraid, but you must fight the foe nonetheless.
2. *Refuse to be a victim.* Do not look for someone to save you or someone else to be the hero. This time, this moment, the hero is you.
3. *Risk is necessary in a crisis.* If this were a normal day-to-day operation, it wouldn't be a crisis. You must learn to trust your gut and take chances, or disaster will win.

Write down how you feel about being brave and taking necessary risks in a crisis.

_____
_____
_____
_____
_____

Lion 3
I Am Not Afraid of What Others Think of Me

1. *Think*: I trust myself and know myself. I need to believe my own truth is worth standing for. If I find out that I am wrong, I can change my mind.
2. *Remember*: Other people may have their own personal agendas and motives, but they have less knowledge of my situation. Why should I value their opinions over my own? I know what's best for myself.
3. *Knowing what others think of me is not fearful.* It is helpful. It can help me understand myself and others better. If people like me, it is because I am authentic, not a people-pleaser, and that is good. If people don't like me, I remind myself that what they think doesn't really matter.

_____
_____
_____
_____
_____

Record your thoughts about the ideas presented in the lion 3 statement.

_____
_____
_____
_____
_____

Lion 4
I Am a Decisive Leader Who Doesn't Give Up

1. *Don't be wishy-washy.* Make up your mind and move forward. If you take too much time to overthink, you will lose the battle.

2. *Lead.* You are in front and must be clear about your objectives. Your followers will respect you if you are determined and directive. Lions don't look back to see if anyone is following. They just do the next right thing based on their own value system.

3. *Never, never give up.* There is always one more idea, one more strategy, one more solution to any challenge.

_____

_____

_____

_____

_____

Evaluate yourself as a leader, an action figure who doesn't hesitate to do what's needed based on the ideas stated above.

_____

_____

_____

_____

_____

CHAPTER 19

FINDING THE FIGHT LION BALANCE

A true lion's heart is rarely challenged. Fight Lions are strong and brave and sometimes formidable. Some people have too much or too little Fight Lion inside. Explore the following ideas to see where you are on the fight lion scale.

The Benefits of Fight

Fight takes immediate action in a crisis. When your fight response activates, you impulsively defend, protect, and stand against danger. You take charge and delegate. You think quickly and clearly without having to plan each detail. You attack the enemy and regain safety as soon as possible. You are a leader or doer who is bold, decisive, and determined. You are often outspoken and confident without questioning whether you will be followed. You do not count the cost but do what is right even when there is the risk of personal danger. You are a rescuer, a hero, a victor, an overcomer. Even when there is no danger, you are proactive and full of energy. You do not sit back and wait for opportunities; you create opportunities. You welcome challenging situations and have a competitive spirit. You do not worry about making mistakes. You just "cut your losses" and move forward.

The Handicaps of Fight

Fight can be intimidating. You may not notice that others have different opinions. You may be insensitive to the individual needs of others. You may have the "big picture" in mind but miss the details that have deeper meaning. You may come across as overbearing and intolerant but will often feel misunderstood, alienated, and lonely. You have good intentions, but others may feel steamrolled in the process. You may be over-reactive and have a penchant for anger and impatience.

Too Much Fight

When you emulate the fight lion skill, you may be seen as arrogant and unapproachable. It may be difficult to have healthy relationships because you always want to be in charge. You are always ready to roar and rule and deflect anyone and anything in your way. You may have a "heart of gold" that is hidden beneath your shaggy mane and towering presence. You are often hot-tempered and quick-witted but have a difficult time blending or bonding.

Too Little Fight

Banning the fight lion from your life can be damaging. Having no fight at all looks timid and wimpy and apathetic. You feel afraid and insecure. You overthink every decision and have so much patience you never get anything accomplished. You feel weak and ineffective and wonder why life seems to pass you by. You wonder why other people always boss you around and don't ask for your opinions.

A Healthy Fight Balance

Fight Lion at its best represents great strength under control. This lion is confident and self-aware while noticing that others have strengths as well. When you discover this lion skill inside yourself, you get stronger through the interchange of powerful ideas and opinions. You acknowledge that you are not always right, but you don't feel defeated when life is challenging. You learn to share the limelight and be a "gentle giant" rather than an arrogant tyrant. Consider the following questions to find your "fight factor."

1. Do you feel a sense of energy and purpose each day? Do you like being you?
    If your answer is yes to both questions, give yourself five points.
    If your answer is no to one question, give yourself six points.
    If your answer is no to both questions, give yourself seven points.
    Your answer: _____
2. Do you notice that others are avoiding you? Do they act as if they expect you to lash out at them?
    If your answer is no to both questions, give yourself five points.
    If your answer is yes to one question, give yourself four points.
    If your answer is yes to both questions, give yourself three points.
    Your answer: _____
3. Do you feel overlooked and discredited? Do you notice that others disregard your opinions?
    If your answer is no to both questions, give yourself five points.
    If your answer is yes to one question, give yourself six points.
    If your answer is yes to both questions, give yourself seven points.
    Your answer: _____
4. Do you think that you always need to be in charge? Do you challenge authority?
    If your answer is no to both questions, give yourself five points.
    If your answer is yes to one question, give yourself four points.
    If your answer is yes to both questions, give yourself three points.
    Your answer: _____

5. Do you see yourself as unprepared and inadequate? Do you often question your own judgment?

>   If your answer is no to both questions, give yourself five points.
>   If your answer is yes to one question, give yourself six points.
>   If your answer is yes to both questions, give yourself seven points.
>   Your answer: _____

6. Are you ready to "save the day" even when no one notices? Do you hold people accountable?

>   If your answer is yes to both questions, give yourself five points.
>   If your answer is no to one question, give yourself six points.
>   If your answer is no to both questions, give yourself seven points.
>   Your answer: _____

7. Are you proud to be strong without having to overpower anyone? Are you willing to share your leadership skills without "lording it over" anyone? Do you restrain your impulse to fight when fighting has no purpose?

>   If your answer is yes to all three questions, give yourself five points.
>   If you believe you deserve more recognition from people, give yourself four points.
>   If you struggle to assert yourself, give yourself six points.
>   Your answer: _____

Your overall fight lion score

Tally up your answers from all seven questions. Then average them by dividing your total score by seven.

1._____ 2._____ 3._____ 4._____ 5._____ 6._____ 7._____
_____ Total divided by seven =_____

Fight Lion
Conclusion/Summary/Recommendations

If your average score is 5, congratulations, you are a super fight lion!

If your average score is less than 5, you may need to cool down the fight in your lion.

Suggestions: Try standing patiently at the end of a line in Walmart. Wait for someone to offer their opinion instead of acting on your own. Stop to think about what you're going to say before you say it.
Bottom line: Do anything that will curb your impulse to speak now, act now, and be in charge.

If your average score is more than 5, you may need to empower the sleeping lion inside.

Suggestions: Volunteer to facilitate a group activity. Delegate responsibilities to someone else. Assert your opinion when you suspect there will be disagreement.

Bottom line: Do anything that will force yourself to step up, step out, and be in a position of authority or leadership.

CHAPTER 20

EMPOWERING ALL THE ANIMALS IN YOUR ZOO

Review the following chart that represents both strengths and weaknesses of each animal in your zoo. Think about which qualities you have and which ones you would like to develop. Notice which weaknesses you would like to temper or eliminate. Learn to consider every animal as a resource, a potential aid in any given situation. Learn to think in an all-inclusive way. Do not eliminate the animals you think are less familiar or seldom utilized. Do not revert to your old patterns of overusing certain animals out of habit. It is natural to favor certain animal skills and have less affinity for others. Remember that when we overuse our preferred strengths, weaknesses result. Think about how a chameleon can change its color to blend in with its environment. Like a chameleon, it would be helpful if you could choose the best strategy for each situation. Don't think for a minute that this means you need to fake your colors. It means you can learn to use each skill in a genuine way, choosing the skills that best match the job or challenge. This broader mindset will catapult you forward with more opportunities and more options than you have ever had before.

Summary Chart of All the Animals in Your Zoo		
	Strengths	*Weaknesses*
Freeze Rabbit	Cautious	Terrified
	Patient	Overly accommodating
	Reflective	Ruminating
	Observant	Suspicious
	Mindful	Emotionally stuck
	Calm	Stagnant
	Meditative	Panicky
	Unassuming	Overlooked

Follow Dog	Loyal	Submissive
	Reliable	Feels unappreciated
	Hard-working	Driven
	Compliant	Feels disrespected
	Steady/dependable	In a rut
	Predictable/consistent	Boring
	Eager to please	Difficulty setting limits
	Trustworthy	Overly trusting
Bond Kangaroo Joey	Attached	Dependent
	Asks for help	Helpless
	Connected	Loss of self
	Agreeable	Passive
	Harmonious	Timid
	Good companion	Lost when alone
	Affectionate	Clingy
	Grateful	Flattering
Nurture Elephant	Self-sacrificing	Lack of self-care
	Protective	Overly protective
	Compassionate	Enabling
	Provider	Needs to be needed
	Nurturing	Suffocating
	Caregiver	Resentful when unappreciated
	Teacher/advocate	Condescending
Escape Cat	Independent	Detached
	Self-aware	Self-absorbed
	Creative	Distracted
	Daydreamer	In denial
	Self-indulgent	Addiction-prone
	Self-protective	Avoidant
	Escape artist	Deceptive
Fight Lion	Brave	Impulsive
	Outspoken	Arrogant
	Leader	Dominator
	Bold	Threatening
	Decisive	Overbearing
	Proactive/Tenacious	Reactive
	Determined	Intolerant

Animal Application: Examples from My Current Life

Applying these principles to everyday life is a challenge at first, but it can become more natural to you if you stroll through your zoo every day and get acquainted with all your animals. You can learn to utilize the skills most needed in any given situation.

Here are some examples from my current "retired" life.

Osteoporosis diagnosis

Less than six months from my retirement date, my new Oklahoma doctor ordered a bone density scan. Subsequent to that scan, I was diagnosed with osteoporosis! My first reaction was denial. *Escape Cat* encouraged me not to worry about it, to ignore the diagnosis, and pretend it wasn't true. After all, I am not bent over like my grandmother was when she died. I haven't fallen or broken any bones. I don't feel weak or old. Right? I began to have my doubts, and *Freeze Rabbit* told me to stop and think about options. I looked at the facts of the bone density scan and reviewed my history of osteopenia. It is true that I have had some bone density loss in the past. It makes sense that my condition could get worse if I don't do something about it. After that frozen moment of contemplation, *Kangaroo Joey* urged me to ask for help. I made an appointment with my doctor. She suggested I take a shot once every six months since other medication options had already been ruled out for my situation. *Freeze Rabbit* hopped back into my consciousness and cautioned me to think about it before deciding. I left the doctor's office with more questions. I had the option of following the doctor's orders and trusting that her advice was best. That's what *Follow Dog* recommended. On the other hand, *Nurture Elephant* counseled me to do some research and find ways to nurture myself. I read everything I could find about osteoporosis causes and treatments. I decided that weight-bearing exercise was the best option for me. *Fight Lion* pushed me forward. I joined Planet Fitness and have been doing weight-bearing exercises for five months now. I talked to my doctor about my choice, and she was willing to back me up on it if I do a repeat bone density scan a year after the first one.

My animal zoo is there to support me, and I am very happy with the decision they helped me make.

Technology Crisis

Technology is challenging to me. That's the most difficult part of writing this book. There have been two major technology crises in the past few months. The first one was when I accidentally deleted twenty-six pages! The second crisis was when I couldn't get the pages formatted correctly and spent two days trying to get an unwanted column to disappear. Both were traumatizing to me, but I will focus on the first crisis since it was the greater error. I had highlighted the entire document so that I could change the font and the spacing. Then I don't know what I did to delete the whole thing. I must have hit the space bar or something? It just disappeared!

My first response was total shock! I froze in my tracks and found *Freeze Rabbit* there beside me to share the sheer panic of the situation. Somehow *Nurture Elephant* reassured me and encouraged me to believe there had to be a solution. I knew I needed to ask for help, so *Kangaroo Joey* accompanied me as I asked my husband for suggestions. He suggested I hit the undo button, but I had already closed the file, and that button didn't work. There was nothing left in the file! I tried to go into the deleted files to recover it, but there were no files there to recover. *Escape Cat* wanted to run. I thought about giving up on the whole idea and going back to sewing or cooking, anything but working on this computer! I did know I needed to take a break. I needed to step away from the problem, so I put it up for the night and got a decent night's sleep. The next morning, *Follow Dog* wanted me to do a tutorial in Word, so I researched everything I could find. I learned a lot but still didn't recover my document. Finally, *Fight Lion* told me to stop crying and face the issue head-on. I had printed out twenty pages of the documents the day before I deleted it. This gave me a guide for retyping the first twenty pages. Then I had to rethink the next six pages. Finally, *Follow Dog* and *Fight Lion* joined forces. *Fight Lion* gave me the courage and determination to face the challenge of reconstructing all that was lost. *Follow Dog* helped me focus on the task even though it was tedious and painstaking. That victory helped me face the second technology challenge and made it clear to me that I always need a backup copy of everything I do.

Animal Application
Your Examples

I am sure that you have been thinking of your own examples, and you have become quite familiar with all the animals in the "zoo of you." Use the following space to write a few of your own adventures.

_____

_____

_____

_____

_____

_____

_____

_____

_____

_____

_____

_____

_____

_____

_____

_____

_____

_____

CHAPTER 21

....

THE FREEDOM IN BROKEN CRUTCHES, MY TESTIMONY

Learning to break the crutches of the past has helped me to remember that God has a plan for my life. He has provided this zoo full of animals to guide me, to give me the ability to "walk without crutches" in this new life of retirement and beyond. The crutches held me back from being dependent on God for my strength. This animal zoo has taught me there is no substitute for God's strength and providence. The more I try to control and master the skills of each animal, the more I fall on my face and see my need, my powerlessness.

I feel like Paul as he wrote in Romans 7:15–25 (ESV).

> For I do not understand my own actions. For I do not do what I want, but I do the very thing I hate. Now if I do what I do not want, I agree with the law, that it is good. So now it is no longer I who do it, but sin that dwells within me. For I know that nothing good dwells in me, that is, in my flesh. For I have the desire to do what is right, but not the ability to carry it out. For I do not do the good I want, but the evil I do not want is what I keep on doing. Now if I do what I do not want, it is no longer I who do it, but sin that dwells within me. So, I find it to be a law that when I want to do right, evil lies close at hand. For I delight in the law of God, in my inner being, but I see in my members another law waging war against the law of my mind and making me captive to the law of sin that dwells in my members. Wretched man that I am! Who will deliver me from this body of death? Thanks be to God through Jesus Christ our Lord! So then, I myself serve the law of God with my mind, but with my flesh I serve the law of sin.

This is good; this is hopeful. This is all about grace. It is true that my animal zoo is a model representing skills that I can practice and learn to use. I have indicated that you can learn to use them as well. Unfortunately, simplistic solutions only work in simple situations. The truth is that life is complicated, and there are no "cookie cutter" answers. The problem is that I forget and fall back to my old habits. Another problem is that I don't like change. I like doing things the way I've always done them even if I do make mistakes. The other most obvious problem, which really isn't a problem at all, is that God made us all different in very special ways. So it's hard for someone who has Follow Dog tendencies to use Fight Lion skills, for example. We're just created to have certain temperaments and develop personalities based on those temperaments. What I'm trying to say is that I like my "zoo of you" model. It's very helpful and gives me insight and an increased awareness of options I wouldn't think about otherwise. The reality of it is that no model can fix our human frailties. We are all broken, powerless to fix ourselves. That's why we need to go back to the beginning, to God, our Creator. Only God, through Christ Jesus, has the power and the love to heal all the brokenness. That's what Paul was talking about in those verses. It's good; it's hopeful. It's all about grace.

Further reflection reminds me of Noah and all the animals in his ark.

> And Noah and his sons and his wife and his sons' wives with him went into the ark to escape the waters of the flood. Of clean animals, and of animals that are not clean, and of birds, and of everything that creeps on the ground, two and two, male and female, went into the ark with Noah. (Genesis 6:7–9)

Can you imagine how Noah must have felt, cooped up with all those animals on the ark for a year? It must have been noisy and uncomfortable. He had to trust God to tell him how to care for the animals and how to be patient until it was time to get out of the ark. Eventually, the rain stopped, the flood waters subsided, and the very first rainbow was created—a promise that there would never again be total destruction of the world by a global flood.

In my imaginary zoo, I have only six animals: a rabbit, a dog, a kangaroo joey, an elephant, a cat, and a lion. It's not nearly as challenging as what Noah had to face, yet it is difficult to figure out how to manage all these animals, especially when they aren't just animals. They are representations of different competing forces inside me that don't seem to cooperate with each other. Some of them may get overfed, underwatered, neglected, or pampered. I tend to have favorite animals at the exclusion of others. How can I keep them all healthy and ready to do their jobs? How do I decide which animal will walk with me each day? It's one thing to break all the crutches, but I don't want any animals to get hurt in the process.

Like Noah, I must defer to God to let me know what to do and how to care for these animals. They are His creation, and I am not equipped to oversee them without His guidance. I will wait for Him to show me the way. I will stop trying to lock the gates and train the animals my way. I must let Him lead me, and the animals, through life. That gives me the freedom to enjoy the animals and to care for all of them without favoring any one above another. It gives me the freedom to be myself and to make mistakes without the fear of punishment. He will pick me up and offer me His wisdom and His grace, His promise for more days of discovery, not destruction.

CHAPTER 22

....

THE CROSS OF CHRIST, NO MORE CRUTCHES, NO MORE BROKENNESS

From the beginning of this book, I've been talking about crutches—defense mechanisms that help us get through trauma and obstacles in our lives. These crutches, when transformed into skills, can help us be proactive, to catch ourselves from falling, before we need more crutches. No matter whether we use reactive crutches or proactive skills, there is still brokenness in our lives. No matter how healthy our zoo animals are, they can still get sick or wounded. Their skills are still inadequate. The "zoo of you" is a tool, but it's not enough. God has the only solution. He sent Himself through Jesus to heal all the wounds, to reconnect us to His love and power. We are incomplete and will always be broken without Him.

> He Himself bore our sins in his body on the cross, so that we might die to sins and live for righteousness. By His wounds you have been healed. For you were like sheep going astray, but now you have returned to the Shepherd and Overseer of your souls. (1 Peter 2:24–25 NIV)

Right about now, I can hear all my animals barking and snorting and mewing and roaring in protest. They want to be the answer, the perfect zoo. They believe they have all the skills and strategies to fix our traumas and problems. They actually do work hard and have very good intentions. The problem is that they can't fix human nature. We humans must be healed before their skills can work. We need divine intervention. That's why it still takes Jesus; it still takes grace. Then the skills and the good works make sense. Then our animals can bark and snort and mew and roar in celebration.

> For by grace you have been saved through faith. And this is not of your own doing; it is the gift of God, not a result of works, so that no one may boast. For we are His workmanship, created in Christ Jesus for good works, which God prepared beforehand, that we should walk in them. (Ephesians 2:8–10 ESV)

So how do we get that divine healing? First, we admit our powerlessness, that we are broken and that we've messed-up. We have to admit we need rescuing before we can get rescued. Then we must believe that God is who He says He is, that He created us, loves us, and has the power to redeem us. We must believe that He sent Himself through Jesus to die for our sins and that He resurrected Jesus from the grave. That means He took our place, and we don't have to die a spiritual death. Jesus offers us His gift of eternal life. By accepting this gift, we receive the Holy Spirit to guide us and help us get through each daily trial. The Holy Spirit is God within us, so we don't have to rely on human means, or the "zoo of you" to rescue us. It's okay when we feel weak, or make mistakes, or choose the wrong animal skill for the job at hand. We're not alone, and we don't have to rely on our own strength anymore.

> But He said to me, "My grace is sufficient for you, for my power is made perfect in weakness." Therefore I will boast all the more gladly of my weaknesses, so that the power of Christ may rest upon me. For the sake of Christ, then, I am content with weaknesses, insults, hardships, persecutions, and calamities. For when I am weak, then I am strong. (2 Corinthians 12:9–10 ESV)

"Learning to walk without crutches" has been an exercise in the discipline of waiting and remembering—remembering the strength God had already given me, remembering that He made this promise He would never forget. Now I can "run and not be weary." There will be many times in the future when I will feel weak or sick or afraid, but I know that He will always be there, lifting me up on eagle's wings.

He has given me this virtual zoo to use as a tool when I need to reflect, remember, and regroup. The animal skills will be at my side to help me see Him working out His purpose. He gave me the insight to create the "zoo of you" so I could get back to the center of my relationship with Him. I pray that He will give you the help and the direction you need to throw away the crutches of this world so you can "run and not be weary."

> But they who wait for the Lord shall renew their strength; they shall mount up with wings like eagles; they shall run and not be weary; they shall walk and not faint. (Isaiah 40:31 ESV)

CONCLUSION

It's hard to believe that I retired one year ago today. I asked myself how I have changed during the past year. It may sound like a cliché, but my only answer is that "I love my life!" This animal journey has helped me immensely. I have gotten used to traveling with the "zoo of me."

Here is a list of highlights from my journey over the past year.

- Freeze Rabbit has helped me to be content wherever I wake up each day, whether it is in New Mexico or Oklahoma.
- Follow Dog has shown me that I can choose to follow wisely, without resentment or regret.
- Bond Kangaroo Joey has helped me to renew my bonds with family. My heart is softer toward my husband and all of my family. Through the distance, I've found a deeper connection I appreciate even more when we can visit face-to-face.
- Nurture Elephant has helped me to see that I can still be compassionate and caring even if I don't have a counseling job.
- Escape Cat has had lots of fun teaching me to renew my interests in reading, sewing, crocheting, and music.
- Fight Lion has encouraged me to be brave. I took two trips by myself and enjoyed flying alone.

My zoo is becoming a permanent part of me. I hope the zoo of you is beginning to flourish as well! Thank you for taking this journey with me.

Now that you have completed the exercises in this book, it's time to take the test again. See if you have been practicing a greater variety of animal skills. I realize that awareness of the different skills has made me consider using them more often. Yes, I still have certain preferences, but now I realize I don't have to be stuck in a rut or crippled by a crutch. I have all the animals at my disposal, ready to take me on new adventures.

THE ZOO OF YOU SKILL
QUESTIONNAIRE, CONTINUING

1. Are you more likely to be
   a. attached and connected (Bond Kangaroo Joey)
   b. brave and outspoken (Fight Lion)
2. Do you see yourself as
   a. a nurturing caregiver (Nurture Elephant)
   b. a proactive leader (Fight Lion)
3. Are you more
   a. loyal and reliable (Follow Dog)
   b. calm and patient (Freeze Rabbit)
4. Are you more
   a. independent and self-aware (Escape Cat)
   b. bonded to one special person (Bond Kangaroo Joey)
5. Are you more likely to be
   a. bold and decisive (Fight Lion)
   b. non-assertive and trusting (Bond Kangaroo Joey)
6. Are you more likely to be
   a. steady and dependable (Follow Dog)
   b. protective and comforting (Nurture Elephant)
7. Are you more likely to
   a. ask for help (Bond Kangaroo Joey)
   b. freeze in a crisis (Freeze Rabbit)
8. Are you more likely to be
   a. a helpful teacher (Nurture Elephant))
   b. a creative daydreamer (Escape Cat)
9. Are you more likely to be
   a. reflective and observant (Freeze Rabbit)
   b. hard-working and compliant (Follow Dog)
10. Are you more likely to be
    a. determined and focused (Fight Lion)
    b. consistent and trustworthy (Follow Dog)

11. Are you more likely to
    a. go on a vacation to de-stress (Escape Cat)
    b. work first/play later (Nurture Elephant)
12. Would you rather be
    a. invisible (Freeze Rabbit)
    b. in the spotlight (Escape Cat)

Count how many answers you chose for each animal prototype.

Freeze Rabbit _____Bond Kangaroo Joey _____Escape Cat _____
Follow Dog _____Nurture Elephant _____Fight Lion _____

ABOUT THE AUTHOR

Brenda R. Abercrombie is a retired professional counselor who wants to continue to share her insights and inspirations through writing books. She grew up in New Mexico, attended Warren Wilson College in Swannanoa, North Carolina, and went on to teach second grade in Lordsburg, New Mexico. She received her master's degree in guidance and counseling from Western New Mexico University in Silver City, New Mexico.

Her primary focus for fifteen years was to be a stay-at-home mom. After that fifteen-year sabbatical, she had a successful twenty-eight-year counseling career. She is a licensed professional clinical mental health counselor and licensed alcohol and drug abuse counselor. Currently, she is happily married to her husband of forty-four years, has four married adult children, and eight grandchildren. She lives in Duncan, Oklahoma, and enjoys fishing, singing, sewing, and visiting grandchildren when she is not writing.

Printed in the USA
CPSIA information can be obtained
at www.ICGtesting.com
JSHW060210030124
54697JS00018B/241

9 798891 121072